NORWAY
SWEDEN
VINLAND
LENINGRAD
MOSCOW
SOVIET UNION
KUBAN AREA
OMSK
TATARSK
NOVOSIBIRSK
Slavgorod
ERKUTSK
L. BAYKAL
BLAGOVESHCHENSK
ZEYA R.
AMUR R.
TSITSIHAR
HARBIN
SAKHALIN
JAPAN
YOKOHAMA
KOREA
MONGOLIA
CASPIAN SEA
ARAL SEA
RAN
AFGHANISTAN
PAKISTAN
CHINA

Seams Of Gold

The Life Of Agnes Warkentin Rice

As Told To

Vera Jones

Fairway Press
Lima, Ohio

SEAMS OF GOLD

SECOND PRINTING 2005

FIRST EDITION

Library of Congress Catalog Card Number: 2005931034

ISBN 0-7880-2149-4

PRINTED IN U.S.A.

In Memory of Agnes and Aron Warkentin
who, with God as their guide and comfort,
had the faith to pick up their family
and leave their home
for freedom to worship God
and live in a free country

Acknowledgments

I am grateful to my father, Aron Warkentin, who risked his life to smuggle his journal out of Siberia and write in it as the events happened. I am also grateful to my mother, Agnes Wiebe Warkentin, who added other family information to my father's journal, and to my nephew, John Schmidt, who provided us with the English translation. I am grateful for the translation of the German lyrics of my father's music by Elsie Enns, of British Columbia, Canada, and Pastor Donald Leckrone, of Antwerp, Ohio. I thank the Heinrich Schultz family of Canada for contributing letters that my father sent to them during the period of time the book covers. I am grateful to my sisters, Helen Hilty and Alice Frey, and my brother, John, and his wife, Myrna Warkentin, who shared their experiences with us, and to my brother, Jake Warkentin, whose tapes of his memories were also added to the book. The text of the memorial service for my mother was given to us by Pastors Ellen and Dean McGormley of Monroe, Michigan. Alice Wilson did proofreading for us, and many relatives and friends provided their encouragement and support. Thank you, also, to Robert G. Jones, who provided a computer and computer assistance.

Table Of Contents

Prologue

A thin, tired woman looked out her back kitchen window and saw her two small daughters dragging their blanket through the field behind the snow-filled garden.

"Alice, Lydia, you're getting the blanket I made you dirty!" she called out the door, but they were well on their way across the field. She grabbed her black shawl, and threw it around her shoulders.

She caught up with them at the cemetery where they were placing the blanket over a grave marked by a stone inscribed with the name, Aron Warkentin. Snow swirled around the girls, and wind caught up their long, blond hair.

"It's cold! We need to keep Papa warm!" said Alice, the taller of the two.

After discovering the blanket on her husband's grave several times, their mother returned one day and replaced it with a coverlet she had made by sewing several pieces of burlap together. Anchoring its four corners with rocks, against the wind's force, she said a brief, "Thank you," to the man whose faith in God's guidance had brought them to this safe place in a new land.

In the third row from the bottom, my mother, Agnes, is fifth from the left and her sister, Anna, is seventh. Their husbands are behind them. Lena and I are third and fourth in the row of girls, and Johan and Jake are fourth and fifth in the front row.

Chapter 1

Not Even My Doll?

"Neta, settle down, and come here immediately. All you children come," my father called one morning. "I have something to tell you." He was wearing his Sunday clothes, which looked strangely tight on him.

"Papa, we're playing a game, and I'm it. They're hiding and I have to find them."

"Well, good. Please go find them, quickly. It's important."

Two-year-old Johan was easy to find, as he was crying. Lena, our older sister, had hidden him behind a door.

"What's to cry about? Go to Papa, he's waiting for us," I instructed, and he ran off to find Papa.

I discovered Lena hiding under the window seat in the parlor, nose in her book. But Jake was harder to find. Finally, noticing the kitchen rug was out of place, I removed the loose boards and found him under the floor in our secret storage area.

"You know we're not allowed to open this," I scolded. "What if someone had come?" As he rose from the hole, I laughed, "Jake, you look like a ghost!"

"Brush me off!" he commanded, although only four.

"A sour ghost," I added, and I swatted him on the back side, as flour flew out from all sides.

"Not so hard!" he scowled.

"Yes, your Majesty." I laughed, making a bow. I took his hand and hurried him to our waiting father, Lena and Johan already by his side.

Once gathered around Papa, we looked like peas in a pod, all blue-eyed with straight blond hair, Lena and mine in braids tied up around our heads, Johan and Jake's cut short. Our clothes were all of the same cloth. Material was cheaper by the bolt, and Mennonite families believed it wasn't how you looked on the outside, but on the inside that counted.

Papa announced, "We're leaving today, and we won't be coming back. Russia is no longer a safe place for us. We will find a new home in a land that will be safe and free. Put on as many of your clothes as you can, but carry nothing in your hands." He stood straight, as always, shoulders back.

"Not even my doll?" I asked unbelieving.

"Not even your doll," he answered sadly. "All must be left behind."

Only my mother had known ahead; the rest of us were stunned. We would be leaving the only place I remembered living, the wood frame, plastered brick farmhouse where I had been born, as had my brothers. It had been our schoolhouse after our village school had been shut down by the Communists. We would also be leaving my Grandmother Wiebe, who lived nearby, and my Grandmother Warkentin, who had lived with us all my life. Both thought they were too old to travel the long distance we planned to go. All my friends and toys, all our belongings would be left behind, even the graves of our brothers, Aron and Gerhard, who had died as babies.

With our mother's help, we put on layers of clothes, three sets being the limit we could manage. I couldn't help but notice the worried look on her pretty, heart-shaped face, and sensed she did not completely agree with Papa in what we were about to do. Her brown hair pulled straight back, accentuated her expression.

Days before our journey, Mama had rolled our bills into narrow strips and sewn them into the seams of our clothes, like seams of gold hidden in the dark folds of the Siberian mountains. Each of us children was carrying with us the wealth of our family in the layers of our clothing now on our backs.

In our pockets was some dry bread she gave us to eat on the train. Somehow, my mother managed to hide under her shawl, a sack with teapot, tea leaves, and a supply of flour. Along the way, she would mix a little flour with boiling water, set it out to dry, and that was the bread we would eat later. Our supply of tea would be replenished with weeds from the Russian prairie. Papa carried the Bible and a small journal hidden in his clothes.

Although we did not know ahead we would be leaving, Lena and I knew why. For many nights, we had gone to sleep knowing that soldiers went at random to villagers' doors while we slept, dragged them from their beds, and forced them to watch while their children were shot and buried, dead or alive in trenches dug by fellow villagers, who also would have been shot if they had refused to do so. Isaac Miller, the father of one of our friends, had been stripped, doused with water, and left to freeze. Heinrich Closson had been sent to a work camp and never heard from again. These punishments were done to force us to give up our allegiance to God, and become Communists.

We set out from our village of Reinfeld, Slavgorad County, on the west Siberian plains, on November 7, 1928, leaving a pot of food on the hearth, dishes laid out on the table, and animals to be fed in their stalls. Although neighbors had secretly bought the stock and the farm, it had to look as if we would be returning to finish preparing the evening meal. Our family could not travel all together, as it would look suspicious, so we would travel in small groups, which included not only my parents, 11-year-old sister, Lena, short for Helene, and my two little brothers, but also, aunts, uncles, and cousins, who would join us along the way. My mother was expecting her fifth child in three months. I, Neta, short for Aganetha, and named after my mother, was 9, and loved adventure. Still, it was not easy leaving.

After tears and good-byes, my cousin, Gerhard Ewerd, had driven us in his wagon pulled by oxen across the plains as far as the village of Gortiez. The next day, we went on to Slavgorad. As we approached the train station there, I could see through the blustery snow, the long, hissing train stretched out along the track, surrounded by the color and movement of travelers. Gerhard helped us out of the wagon, and we waited while Papa bought tickets to Blagoveshchensk, 1,880 miles east of us; but first we had to go west to Tatarsk, to meet up with the Trans-Siberian Railroad. When people we knew saw us there and asked us where we were going, we said, "to the Kuban area," in the west near the Black Sea, where our ancestors had first settled in Russia.

Gerhard exchanged hugs with us, and wished us luck. Papa later wrote in his diary, "Our thoughts were already out in the wide world. We wondered what life might have in store for us." Ewerd waved as Papa led us up the dripping steps of the train, his high, handmade boots glistening with snow. It was 7 in the evening, November 8.

The coach we entered was a noisy place, passengers gathering in groups, sharing food they had brought, and drinking tea from a pot atop a simmering samovar. I spotted the familiar face of my favorite uncle, Abram Schmidt. He had a long, handsome face with a white moustache, two right triangles that met at his long nose. He had dark eyes, and skin darker than the rest of ours. Distinguished was a good word for him. He had been born in the Ukraine, and had often fueled our imaginations with imitations of wild bears and Siberian tigers, and we had been delightfully scared.

Aunt Anna, resembling our mother, sat beside him, surrounded by boys, 3-year-old Neil, on her lap, who became "a bruising Purdue Boilermaker halfback" in the '40s; Abram, 10; Peter, 8; and Johan, 5, standing around them. Jake and Johan were excited to see them. Like my mother, Aunt Anna was expecting her fifth child. Lena and I hoped our mother and aunt would have girls this time.

The Schmidt family had come to Slagorod on their own, on November 6, and stayed overnight, as our leaving Reinfeld all together would have looked suspicious. We greeted each other, and our lively group became still livelier with four boys added to our number. Uncle Abe handed Mama a box wrapped in gold paper.

"Here, Neta, pass out the chocolates, and we'll have tea." He lowered his voice, so that only we could hear, "Our adventure has begun!"

Uncle Abe before his mustache turned white

Uncle John Warkentin in Siberia

Chapter 2

We Drew Straws And I Was Chosen To Go

When the train finally started, with heaving and jerking, and shouts of the crew, we children learned the difficulty of maneuvering about in a moving train. Frightened at first, we eventually learned to trust the engineer to keep the train on the track, and get us where we were headed, safely. I learned to love the rocking of the train at night, the steady clacking of wheels on ties, lulling me to sleep.

Once settled into a routine on the train, my mother had time to think about the irreversible steps we were taking, and the dangers ahead. I overheard her talking with my father, "We lost tiny Aron and Gerhard before they even had a chance to live a year. I can't stand the thought of losing the other children, too. What we're trying is impossible! We'll be caught and killed!" she cried, "or we'll starve to death. Better to die at home than on a hopeless journey." A tear escaped down her strained face. Back then, mothers often lost a child during childbirth or due to disease, and that child was locked in the heart and never forgotten. Aunt Anna, too, had been crying.

"Aganetha, God will take care of us. God told me what to do," my father said calmly. In fact, as I was to learn later, my father and his brother, Isaak Warkentin, had been preparing for two years for our escape from Russia. Ever since a boy my father had helped warned him that his name was posted as due for Communist investigation, Papa had been planning our leaving. His sister and my mother's sister and their famiies had emigrated to Canada earlier in the 1920s. The families corresponded continually, and my father wrote and asked advice about emigration. By 1927, when my parents had decided to go, emigration was no longer permitted. By then, 2,000 Mennonites had already left.

The plan for our leaving began with my father and uncles quietly selling all they owned, as they would need every penny they could get for the trip. So great was the villagers' respect for my father, that, even though they could not afford the trip themselves, there was no question that my father could trust them to be silent about what he was planning to do. He had been a leader in the community, not only setting up a school in our home against Communist dictates, but also helping distribute food during the Great Famine of 1919-1925. Our home had been a central point from which food donated by Mennonites in the United States had been distributed to our neighbors and fellow villagers.

In the summer of 1928, my father and Uncle Isaak traveled to Blagoveshchensk, a town 1,880 miles east on the Trans-Siberian Railroad. Nearby, at the village of Amur, on the Amur River, which is the boundary line between Siberia and Manchuria, the two brothers had built a hunting cabin. Aunt Helene and our cousins, and another cousin, Jakob Weibe from Nikolaipol near Reinfeld, had gone to stay there with them after the cabin was built. The men and Jacob, 17, had hunted and trapped all summer and fall. Then my father had returned to our home to prepare us for leaving. If we should be stopped along the way, we could explain that we were going to visit relatives near Blagoveshchensk. The authorities would recognize my father as one of the hunters there the previous summer. My father and Uncle Isaak had made plans for the time we would reach the cabin in the east. We children knew nothing of those plans. Looking back, I realize we suspected something. There was Mama's extra sewing, our parents' hushed talking, and the sense of urgency they seemed to have in doing ordinary tasks. Not until after leaving home, however, did those things make sense.

The train stopped at Tatarsk at noon, November 9, and from a vendor, we were able to buy kabob, chunks of lamb and onions that had been charcoal broiled on sticks. Another vendor sold us broiled beets that steamed in the cold air, and were eaten with yogurt. We had to wait there, for another train, so we could travel east to Blagoveshchensk. We two families sat outside with our eight children because it was so crowded in the waiting room, and none of us wanted to go inside, even though it was somewhat cool.

While we waited there, we children became restless, so Uncle Abe said to us, "If you can sit and listen, I will tell you a story."

We all became quiet, because he had to talk softly so as not to be heard by others.

"Tell us the one about the night you spent in a hog house," begged Lena, who knew a lot of his stories already.

So Uncle Abe began.

"This is a true story that happened before Stalin had come to power, when the country was involved in a civil war, the Red Army and the White Army fighting for dominance. One night, our village was surrounded by the Red Army and no one could leave or enter. No one would turn Communist, so all of the men of our village were taken to the courthouse. One man from each village was forced to go with the Communists to surround another village. We drew straws, and I was chosen to go. When we got there, the White Army, or Bolsheviks, surrounded it, and the Red Army and the White Army fought. I was able to get away during the fighting, and hid in a hog house for not one, but three days. Eventually, I got home safely, and Aunt Anna was so happy to see me, she let me into the house and hugged me in spite of my needing a bath!"

Threshing on the Siberian plains

Chapter 3

There's A Body In The Corncrib!

It was 6 p.m., November 9, when we were once again on our way, this time on a new train, headed east toward Blagoveshchensk. When we were all settled in our seats and the train had pulled out of the Tatarsk train station, Lena and I began to sing, to pass the time, and amuse the smaller ones, until my father, fearing our German language would draw attention to us, told us to stop. The Russian ban on the German language had begun in 1914, when trouble with Germany started. The anti-German movement, due to World War I, meant no German language could be used in the press, or in an assembly of more than three people. Also, German books were burned. We could be fined 300 rubles or put in prison for disobeying. Thus, Mennonites had learned enough Russian to speak to officials when necessary.

The anti-German movement also brought about liquidation of property owned by those of German ancestry. We Mennonites, originally of Dutch background, had sent a delegation to the czar, documenting our Dutch ancestry, and were given immunity from the land liquidation the Germans were being subjected to.

A kind women sitting near Lena and me gave us some yarn and knitting needles so we could knit. We older children had been taught to knit at an early age, and then we taught the younger ones, as they got old enough to learn. Each child in the family was responsible for knitting his own stockings, scarves, and mittens, as he or she grew old enough. We were grateful this time to have something to do.

As our train crossed the Siberian plains, we occasionally passed tiny villages, the farms lined up facing each other along either side of a road, huddled together as if for warmth and protection, and reminding me of our village of Reinfeld. Our farm, like the other Mennonite farms, was attached to the barn by what is known in modern times as a breezeway, so we could reach the animals and other storage buildings even in the deepest snow or worst blizzard. Also, the animals' bodies added warmth to our set of buildings.

"Lena," I asked, "do you remember the time we were playing, and came across the dead body in the corncrib?"

She nodded, "That was a shock, wasn't it? Why didn't they warn us?"

"We weren't supposed to be playing near the corncrib, remember? Imagine how uncomfortable that would be, a bed of hard corn as your last resting place."

"Well, they did bury him properly in spring when the ground thawed!"

Cowchip fuel and wood were kept in our passageway, and food was stored in an underground cellar for winter use. There was a shed where we kept ground corn and wheat from our own village mill. The Mennonites were prosperous and envied by the Communists. Their soldiers looked on our farms as sources of free food and supplies. Also, the soldiers of both the White and Red armies often found temporary quarters by moving in on Mennonite families. Fortunately, we never had to provide them with lodging.

As I looked out at others' homes, I began to realize that I no longer had a home, but I could not picture any other way of living. I thought back to my days of work on the farm. Since we girls were oldest, we helped our father hand plow, hand plant, weed, and hoe. To thresh the wheat, the Mennonites invented a machine run by horse power. Helen got to ride the horse, because she was taller, while I held the reins and walked the horse around in a circle. Soldiers came as we were threshing, and held their bags out to collect the grain as it came out of the machine. I remember my father "breaking" the machine by removing the bolt from the lug, and after the soldiers left, "fixing" the machine so we could go on with our threshing. The soldiers couldn't understand why we Mennonites had so much trouble with our machine, but they didn't know how to fix it. We did not understand why they would take all the grain, leaving us no seed for the next season. It only meant they would have no crop to steal from us at the next harvest.

The soldiers not only took grain, seed, and food, they took clothes, work horses, even the pillows from our davenport to cushion their saddles. As I remember my mother saying, "The Reds held a sack under everything!"

She even took our outgrown clothes and remade them to fit, as we grew older, or remade them for the younger children. Every scrap had to be saved and used.

"You're wearing my old dress today," Lena would tease, "I wore it when it was new."

"But it looks a lot better on me!" I would answer.

Likewise, I became used to seeing my old dresses become Jakob's and Johan's shirts or reappear as patches in our quilts.

Hand-me-down clothes seemed a trivial thing, after we had seen a prison work camp from the train window, when we were nearing the city of Novosibirsk. The czars had originally exiled their enemies to work camps in Siberia, and now Stalin was building them all along the Trans-Siberian Railroad. Dark, wooden structures in the cold, white setting of the Siberian winter, they were surrounded by walls of wood and metal, with fences of barbed wire, and guarded by soldiers with police dogs. It was an eerie scene in the November moonlight . We had friends in the prison in Omsk, not far east of our home; their lives had been frozen in time for committing no crime.

Political enemies of Stalin, but also scientists, artists, writers, even many Communist Party officials, were sent to these prisons; at least those who were not shot to frighten the others. Anyone who disagreed with Stalin or those he just disliked, became a member of the Gulag, his system of "lags" or camps. It was said in later years, that he killed so many army officers, that he hadn't enough generals in his army when World War II began. He sent 17-25 million to labor camps from 1928 until 1953, when he died. They worked in the factories, or on the railroads, dug canals, and laid roads, farmed, or worked in the many mines in the Siberian mountains. Many of those prisoners died of tuberculosis, malnutrition, execution, or just from long hours and the extreme cold, sometimes colder than -40 degrees F. Many were buried together anonymously in pits.

"Thank you God," I silently prayed, "for guiding us on our journey." We could be thrown into prison or killed for leaving the country illegally, and just the discovery of the German Bible Papa had hidden in his clothes could cost him his life. The year 1929 was going to be the end of the Five Year Plan, and everyone in Russia was to declare loyalty to the Communist Government. If we stayed, we would be forced to do so or be imprisioned or killed.

In the early morning of November 10, as our train came out of a dense forest and crossed the bridge over the River Ob, we began to see smoke curling from moonlit cabins; and soon we arrived at the train station at Novosibirsk. Once again the waiting room was full, so as it became light, we took a horse-drawn cab through the snow into the city. Many people there were wearing shapkas, round brimless hats made of sable, mink, muskrat, and even wildcat fur.

"This is a city of trappers, hunters, and miners," said Papa, as we walked around to shops and bought dried reindeer meat, smoked cheese, and dried cranberries. From babushkas, Russian for "grandmothers," we bought flat bread and tea on the street, and some other necessary items we had had to leave behind when we left home. Papa said the people call the River Ob, "Babushka," because like a slow-moving, wise, old woman, it provides so much for them. We returned to the station and spent the night on the train. Papa wrote in his journal that night, " Along with thc cab driver, we had to pay a porter, since we had so many things. Altogether, our day in Novosibirsk cost us 6 rubles." In the midst of all dangers, Papa calmly kept accounts of every ruble spent, showing faith that there would be need for our money in the new life to follow.

Chapter 4

There Are Hidden Treasures

On the evening of November 10, we left Novosibirsk in a very nice coach on train number four, third class. As the train pulled out of the station, and wound into the countryside, we began to see more and more mountains stretching up into the clouds.

"Under these mountains," Papa told us, "treasures are hidden, seams of gold, copper, iron, coal, and even oil. The trees you see are treasures, too, larch, pine, hemlock, spruce, and birch. They are cut, and become houses, furniture, and toys. And someday, on our trip, you might see another treasure, the beautiful Siberian tiger, the largest of all living cats," Papa continued, "so majestic and powerful an animal!"

"Will it sound like Uncle Abe?" I asked.

"It will do a good imitation of Uncle Abe," he laughed.

I looked for days, from then on, but never saw one, just snow, always snow.

Papa told us we were in a river valley made by the river cutting through the mountains over thousands of years. "It has made a path for our train as it has for traders and soldiers and settlers who live here. At Blagoveshchensk, where we are going, it joins another river and the two become the larger, Amur River."

"Where does all the water come from to make the rivers?" I wondered.

"Many rivers in Siberia are melted glaciers and snow," Papa answered, "but the Amur is made of rain. At certain times of the year, there are heavy rains called monsoons that used to flood the valley. Now there are dams to control it and let it go a little at a time."

As our train approached the city of Irkutsk, the unofficial capital of Siberia, we got a view of the city. Besides the onion domes of Chistianity, there were the minarets of Islam rising through the frigid winter sky. Stalin had not yet destroyed those outer religious structures, but his work camps were evidence of his attempts to destroy the living religions within those structures.

Our train stopped for three hours. Papa got off the train to send a telegram to Uncle Isaak at Blagoveshchensk to ask him to meet us at the train station in two days. While he was gone, we saw out the window people with different faces, descendants of Cossack fur traders, European faces of descendants of exiles from tsarist oppression, the Asian faces of indigenous tribes of Northern Siberia, and Buryats or Buddhists in pointed fur caps, who were now also being persecuted. Stalin eventually destroyed nearly all their temples in the area east of Irkutsk around Ulan Ude, originally Mongolian territory. We Mennonites were one people of many being persecuted for their religious beliefs.

To my dismay, I also saw men dressed in the much-feared uniforms of the Communist soldiers, waiting to board the train.

"Lena, we'll be caught and tortured for running away. We'll never make it out. They're too strong for us."

"Quiet, they'll hear you! God will make us even stronger!" she comforted me. I remembered back in Reinfeld, our encounter with soldiers similarly dressed one Sunday as we had returned from church at a neighbor's home. As we had approached and seen horses outside, our father had said to Mama, "Quick, hide our girls in the garden, so the soldiers won't know they're here."

As the rest of my family entered our home, the soldiers were eating our roast, from the black kettle on the hearth. They ate all they could, and then spat on what was left; then they forced my family to eat it.

"Do you have any sisters?" one of the soldiers asked my little brothers, Jakob and Johan, but neither of them said a word. Their silence spared Lena and me from being raped that Sunday afternoon. My father said afterward: "God put his hand on those little fellows' mouths." Lena and I wished God would quiet them more often.

Besides us girls, there were other things hidden from the soldiers' eyes, like one of those pictures in children's magazines where the reader has to find things hidden in uncustomary places. Cabbages, carrots, and potato skins sliced thickly with eyes still on them, were hidden under the dirt floor of our living room and bedroom. The dirt smoothed over and whitewashed, concealed our winter supply of vegetables and the beginning of the next year's potato crop. Inside our straw mattresses was seed for spring planting and feed for our animals. I was glad we did not have to sit anywhere near the soldiers after they boarded our train, as we were still hiding a great deal from them.

My father returned safely to the train, bringing with him delicious salmon-like fish called omul, for us to eat; and soon afterward, the train left the station. After a while, we went through a tunnel in the mountain and came out beside an enormous body of water partially frozen and gleaming in the sunlight. The wind was very strong and pushed against the train window.

"Papa," I asked, "is that the ocean?"

"No," Papa explained, "that is Lake Baykal, called the Frozen Pearl of Siberia. It is the home of the omul we had for dinner. If you look carefully, you may also see nerpa, a kind of seal that live here. This is the deepest lake in the world, over one mile deep and 395 miles long. It contains over 1/5 the world's fresh water. Sometimes it freezes to five feet thick by January. Before the track was built around it, the train cars used to be dragged across the ice by horses when the lake was frozen solid. When it was not frozen, the train cars were ferried across on boats."

Papa's soft voice and the movement of the train lulled me to sleep, but it was not peaceful sleep. Papa woke me, and I saw everyone staring at me as I opened my eyes.

"Neta, you were screaming; it's okay, it was just a dream. Not a very good one, eh?"

"Papa," I whispered, clinging to him, "there were the men in the uniforms, the soldiers, they were counting — one, two, three, four. We were number four. They knocked on our door in the night. You opened it and they took you away. Then, there were gun shots and screams! Papa, Papa, are you safe?"

"Yes, little Neta, I am safe. We are leaving to be safe. Our home was not secure, but soon we will find a new home where we will be safe. The soldiers will not come to houses at night and take people away. Here, Communists have the power, but God is more powerful. He will show us where to find a new home so we will live in safety."

Papa then quietly quoted from Psalm 140:

> *Guard me, O Lord, from the hands of the wicked;*
> *Preserve me from violent men,*
> *who have planned to trip up my feet.*
> *Arrogant men have hidden a trap for me,*
> *and with cords they have spread a net,*
> *by the wayside they have set snares for me.*
> (v. 45 RSV)

Papa had written in his journal a number of Bible passages that fit our situation perfectly. Another passge from Psalm 140 was:

> *I know that the Lord maintains the cause of the*
> *afflicted,*
> *and executes justice for the needy.*

Surely, the righteous shall give thanks to Thy name;
the upright shall dwell in Thy presence.
(v. 12-13 RSV)

One of my father's favorite passages was from 2 Corinthians, chapter 4:

We are afflicted in every way, but not crushed;
perplexed but not forsaken,
struck down, but not destroyed. (v. 8-9 RSV)

I asked Papa why he wrote down the amount of money we spent each day.

"Neta," he answered, "It is important to keep track of what you have and what you spend, especially when you have to keep it so well hidden that you may forget, yourself, how much you have and where it is." He winked at me, and I felt proud to be a part of the consiracy to smuggle our money out of Russia.

After our trip had ended, Papa's journal had been stuck away in a cedar chest for years, and only recently brought to light by my brother, Johan, now John, who had it translated from the German language by a professor at Bluffton College, in Ohio. John still has it, with the Bible, and the black shawl Mother wore on the trip.

Life on board the train was not always frightening, nor were we always sad to be leaving our old home. The trip on the train was a rest for Lena and me. We girls were never spared physical work because we were girls. In fact, a man was considered too old to work at the age of 50, but such was not true of their wives, who continued to work until death. On the train, there was no farm work to do, no barn to clean, no animals to milk or feed, and no manure cakes to be made and dried for fuel to heat our house; and we did not have to help with the cooking.

Life back home had not been all work, however, toys had been whittled, and we had made rag dolls, without faces, as it was not thought right to make images on our things; but our imaginations supplied the flashing eyes and bright smiles. One day Lena noticed tears running down my cheeks, and asked why.

"I miss my doll, and old Blossom (our cow), and friends," I wailed much like Johan. I missed school, too, because that's where I saw my friends, first at the village Mennonite school, and then later in our home with Papa teaching us.

"Hush," Lena warned, "we're supposed to be on a holiday, not leaving home forever!"

I asked my sister recently, "Lena (now Helen), now that we have grown old, do you remember our family celebrating Christmas?"

She laughed and said, "Oh, yes, Santa always came and brought us gifts, even when we escaped to China and had very little. And we danced, and Papa played the fiddle. All the neighbors came to join in. Remember, too, there was some vodka in the house!"

Chapter 5

When It Rains, It Pours!

Between Irkutsk and Batchkorova, an axle on the train ahead of us broke, and our train had to wait six hours while it was fixed. The long wait was trying on our patience, and Papa told us stories to pass the time. One of them was about the Great Famine from 1919 to 1925.

"It began the year you were born, Neta," he told me. "There was little to eat, and when anyone had food, occupying soldiers would take it. Each family had a quota of grain to give to the government. Some families starved to death because the quota was the same for all, regardless of the size of the family. Food was so scarce that people ate leaves, bark, cornstalks, and even thistle. They killed cats, dogs, and gophers, and ate dead horses, also. Sometimes, children were so hungry, they would eat unripe greens, and become sick and die."

He told us how the Russian economy had been at a standstill. President Herbert Hoover of the United States had sent food to Russia under the New Economic Policy. In Reedley, California, where many Mennonites had settled after leaving Russia, a Mennonite Central Committee had been founded to send food and clothing to their former Mennonite villages in Siberia. M. B. Fast and W. P. Newfield had escorted the food to Siberia, and set up food kitchens and distribution centers like the one that had been set up in our house with Papa organizing the distribution.

"Do you remember, Neta," he asked, "How we hid food under the floor and seed in the mattresses? That is how we survived the famine. God guided us in out-foxing the soldiers at every turn. We will survive, now, too, in a new land where He is guiding us to go." Papa marveled daily at God's faithfulness; and I marvel even now at my father's confidence in God's care.

We didn't reach Batchkorova until November 17. We waited there a day, left at night, and arrived at Blagoveshchensk on November 18, but Isaak was not there. Father wrote in his journal, "We stood there like oxen before the mountain, and did not know what to do or where to go." He finally rented a wagon and horses, and found us quarters for the night. The next morning, he set out to see if Isaak had come to the station to meet us. Some German people were there, but not Isaak. Papa's journal shows his dismay:

> *The next day, I was so tormented with impatience, that I went at once to look again to see if Isaak had arrived. When I came into the railroad yard, the Germans called, "It is good to see you again. Are you coming to live here? Did you bring your family?" I did not know what to answer. What should I say that would help and not be a lie? And then the thought came to me, as it is written: "When the ox falls into the well, so save him even if it is on Sunday" (Luke 14:5). So I said, "No, I would not drag my family to the Amur. I came alone to put my property in order, and then I will go back to the Kuban to my family."*

Papa never got over having to break a commandment, but knew that he was being guided to do so. We learned that Isaak had had the same experience. When he had come to look for us, he had been asked questions, and hadn't known what to say. At last, he and my father found each other and made plans.

After dark, we left the town in a wagon, so no one would see us. We had four men, two women, and eight children in one wagon. We drove over a bridge above the Zeya River into the next village, and remained there overnight. Early in the morning, we were up and off in a round about way, as if we were going from Bninfa to Pruschup, then to Zaamenka, and then to the city, so that we would not meet anyone who knew us. We drove until evening, when we met a Russian friend who knew what we were doing and would help us. We stayed with him overnight, and in the morning, left the Schmidt family with him. They would follow us later. The rest of us went on to Heinrich Michelson's house. He was a Mennonite who lived near the border between Russia and Manchuria. He helped Mennonites cross the border for a fee. We arrived at Heinrich's house at midnight, and they took us in to warm us, saying they had been expecting us.

We learned then, that the Amur River was not yet completely frozen in all places. We had to cross it to get to Manchuria, and had counted on riding across in sleighs. During the long Siberian winters, the Amur River freezes as deep as six feet or more.

"When it rains, it pours!" moaned Papa. "What do we do now? We have come so far, in great danger, and even lied, and all this for nothing! It appears that freedom is not to be for us after all." It was one of the few times on our trip that he showed discouragement.

"Aron," Mama spoke quietly, "remember in the Bible, how the Red Sea parted for the Israelites as they escaped from Pharaoh's army? And did not the waters of the Jordan stop for them as they crossed the river? Will not God see us safely across, after all He has brought us through?" Papa's eyes grew with amazement, and his mouth hung open, not a word coming out.

Chapter 6

You Have Vanquished The Dragon!

We stayed the night and slept a little. In the morning, Heinrich said, "You men go to your hunting cabin. My brother and I will take the girls and walk them across the river. We have another young boy who can go with us and help. Then, when it is dark, your wife and the little ones can be taken across. You can cross swiftly later, when the river is frozen. You must not be seen with them, or the border guards will know you are escaping from Russia."

My father explained to us girls, "Because the ice is not completely frozen, we cannot all go together in the sleigh. We will have to cross the border a few people at a time, so we will not look like a family leaving the country."

"But Papa," I said, "why don't we wait until the river is frozen and then go together in the sleighs?"

"We may already be missed back home," Papa explained patiently, "and they may be looking for us right now. The longer we stay in Russia, the more dangerous it becomes. I know my girls will be brave. God will go with you. You will be hidden on Heinrich's sister's farm after you cross the river and are in Manchuria. We will meet there when we have crossed. We must fool them all the way," and he hugged us tightly.

On November 22, Heinrich and his brother, Johan, and another boy named Schmitz, took Lena and me down the steep banks through the evergreen trees, to the Amur River. It was a cold day and snowing, but there were dark spots in the river where Father knew the ice was thin; and he was to worry about our safety for hours to come. He not only had to trust in God, but also in Heinrich Michelson. The river, being the boundary line between Russia and Manchuria, was patroled by soldiers constantly, and even if the ice held us, there was the risk of being stopped, and even killed by the Communists. I had been given an ax to carry, and Lena, a saw. When a patrol officer came riding out of the forest and stopped us, Heinrich explained to him, "We are gathering wood," and we were allowed to go on. Only then, did I realize how long I had been holding my breath in fear.

As we gingerly walked on the ice-covered river, avoiding the dark spots, I remembered our walks to school in the heavy snow back home. Sometimes snow was up to the tops of the houses, and we had to leave and return through the roof, using the skylight as a door. "Maybe that's why Santa Claus developed the habit of entering homes through the chimneys," I thought to myself.

Back home, Papa had attached ropes from farmhouse roof to farmhouse roof. As we walked through the snow, we could hold onto the ropes to prevent us from dropping down an air pocket and being buried there until spring. I longed for Papa's lifeline now, but knew his prayers for us, every minute of the way, were as strong as that security rope.

There were islands in the Amur River where we had to clamber up the banks and back down, getting soaked through all our layers of clothes, knowing we had no dry ones to put on at our destination. As we were looking across the ice through a curtain of snow, we saw ahead a series of mountains rising to greet us with a further challenge. If we survived our river trek, we would have to climb over them.

When we had made it across the river, Lena and I were taken to a storage shed to hide until the others had crossed.

"Congratulations! You have vanquished the Black Dragon," Heinrich exclaimed.

"What do you mean?" asked Lena, puzzled.

"To the Chinese, the Amur River is Heilong Jiang, the Black Dragon. The Black Dragon is 2,700 some miles long and sits with its two tails in China, winds around making the boundary between Russia and China, and its mouth lies at the Pacific Ocean." We prayed very hard that the Black Dragon would not swallow our mother and little brothers, who would be taken across later, after dark.

That night, Heinrich, his brother, Jakob, and our Wiebe cousin, 17, also named Jakob, from Nikolaipol, took Mama and our little brothers across. One of the escorts took Jake by the hand, another carried Johan, and the third carried two tablecloths tied up around the few belongings they could carry. Then, Mama followed them.

My father had written in his journal, "What a dark and troubled time it is, but there is no way, only forward."

We had tears, hugs, and laughter to share when Lena and I saw them appear out of the darkness and join us where we had been hidden.

"Neta, look at his mouth!" Lena was pointing at Johan.

"No wonder the crier has been so quiet," I laughed, and grabbed a corner of cloth from between Johan's lips, and pulled. Out of his mouth came Mama's red kerchief.

"So this is why he didn't cry. What a great idea! Too bad it has to be removed." Johan began to cry.

We were taken five miles to the village of Guhna, to the farm of Heinrich's sister, Johan and Jakob with Mother in a sleigh, Lena and I walking. It was a long trek through mountains, but the exercise warmed us. My mother had been in freezing water to her waist on the trip across the river, and upon arrival at the farm, an old Chinese woman predicted that the unborn child would never live, and that my mother would die, also. We learned then that Jakob Wiebe would stay with us, as he, too, was leaving Russia for good.

Papa, still on the Russian side of the river, wrote in his journal that day:

> *I went back to Heinrich's to see if everything went well with my family. When I arrived, they were not yet back from the other side, and the women folk cried. There was not yet any news from them as to whether they had arrived safely, or had the ice broken and they were somewhere under water? So I stayed a while, and then Heinrich and the boys came back with a letter from Lena saying they had all arrived and were well received. So I thought about Noah when he opened the window to let doves out, and they came back with an olive leaf; so it was with the letter. I pondered for a while and wondered what would happen, my family across the water without me, among strangers with whom they could not speak. I stayed with Isaak for six days and always was uncertain, imagining that someone was behind me. I will never feel secure until I have the ones that belong to me, again before my eyes.*

In her letter, Lena had not told our father about our mother's condition.

Those six days seemed like forever, as we waited on that Chinese farm for our Papa. But finally, on November 29 a horseman came riding, dressed from head to toe in a suit of animal skins, a hunter on a shaggy, white horse, gun across his back, and only his eyes and nose showing through a helmet of fur.

"It's Papa!" I screamed and forgetting we were to stay hidden in our straw dwelling, I burst out to meet him and get the first hug from that Cossack hunter, no longer a stranger, as he spoke in his familiar voice, "God has set us free! We are all now out of the power of Communism, and safe and sound."

My mother wrote in my father's diary later, "Thursday, November 29, I saw my Aron again!" She seemed to be all right, and had not lost the unborn baby.

Papa then told us of those six days he had been across the river without us. "I sold the hunting cabin and most of our belongings, shoes, boots, a blanket, and pillows. In crossing the border, anything is too much! Then, taking what was left in a sled pulled by two white horses, I drove away from Shiminovsk as if I would go to the Kuban. I circled and came back to Heinrich's, where I left the rest of our belongings and money. After spending the night there, I hitched up my horses, and Heinrich hitched his two brown ones to his sleigh. The river ice was still thin. I took the gun, and Heinrich took two straw ticks and a comforter. We tied a chamber pot to the front of my sled, and added an axe and skunk traps. Everything needed to look as if we were trappers out on a hunting expedition. We made it across the river safely into Manchuria, and spent the night by the border. The next day we climbed into the mountains, so slow and jolting a trip! Finally, as Heinrich and I approached the farm here, and I saw my little Neta come running to greet me, I knew the long nightmare had ended, and we were safe."

"Papa," Lena said, "Heilong Jiang did not swallow us up!"

"What?" asked Papa.

"The Black Dragon, Papa," I said. "The Chinese have named the river, Black Dragon. The Black Dragon did not swallow us up."

"No, my girls, he did not," and he quoted from Isaiah, chapter 43, verse 2. "Should you pass through the sea, I will be with you, or through the rivers, they will not swallow you up."

I thanked God that night that Papa had made it safely to us, and that the Black Dragon had not swallowed any of us, as we crossed its wide back.

The entry appearing in my father's journal for that day stated, "Good-bye Russia. No longer will we give you money or soldiers. We will live differently, where all have their own free will. None will take advantage of us, and it will be a joy to live. Good-bye, Russia!"

Chapter 7

Under The Haystack, Fast Asleep

All through my life, I had thought we spent those days on the Manchurian farm, hidden under a huge haystack, like "Little Boy Blue" in the nursery rhyme. Now, my sister says it was a cone shaped building with a roof of straw, a storage shed for wheat, perhaps. Food and water were brought to us by kind, Manchurian people who shared all they had with us. Our first hours together, we warmed ourselves and ate, exhilarated by our new freedom; and then we slept for hours. Before leaving the Russian side of the river, we children had been promised candy, and when we arrived at the Manchurian farm, we were disappointed when our candy treat was not given to us. An old woman gave us raisins, instead. She spoke to us in a sing-song language, we would soon become accustomed to hearing, during our stay there.

Our hosts lived a simple communal life, being in a remote area away from town. Their lives, unlike ours in Russia, were the same each day.

"They are like ravens," my father said, "they all have black or gray hair, wear the same dark clothes, and always eat the same food."

For breakfast, they had dumplings and a mixture of vegetables and tea. They did not eat with forks or spoons, but with wooden sticks we had to practice a long time to be able to use. They called the dumplings, *piroshki*, made by mixing flour and water, steaming the mixture over water, and then browning it on sticks over an open fire. In the evening, they made soup, and had leftover *piroshki*. Occasionally, they made a substitute coffee, and had gruel made from groats. They also had pork, sometimes. They seemed to have no rules about food. The men did the cooking, and each day they would bake fresh; only enough was made for the day. If anyone became hungry between the morning and evening meal, he drank tea, which was kept hot all day in a samovar. There was a special grandmother with a long pipe, which she held in her mouth constantly, even while working.

In spite of the lack of variety in their lives, they seemed to expect nothing more. My father noted in his diary, "We hear nothing of prayer or talking with God, and yet they are happy people."

We discovered that food in Manchuria was expensive. For 1 Russian ruble, we got only 40-50 kopecks. Flour cost 3 rubles a pound, meat 20-30 kopecks, and fish, 10 kopecks a pound. The food on the farm was monotonous to us, after what we had been able to buy along the Trans-Siberian Railroad at each stop to eat on the train.

We had brought out of Russia only what could be carried in two tablecloths. Father decided to go back across the border to get some of the things we had left there. So in spite of my mother's pleas, my father and our cousin, Jakob Wiebe, went back across the border on December 4. As they walked, they had plenty of time to think. Papa wrote in his journal later:

> *Jakob and I discussed our fears. Why had we started this trip? What good can come of it? Now, my brothers and sisters and acquaintances, you will think this all happened to me in order for me to learn that the fork sits on the handle; that my life was not good enough for me, and I had to choose to leave. I shall not forget this as long as I live, and when I shall arrive where I plan to be, I shall be satisfied.*

Later he wrote:

> *I would advise none to do the same. The whole thing is like a chess game; when one has luck, he has luck and when not, everything is lost. I imagined that the trip would be terrible, but if I had known it would be so difficult with a family, then I would not have done it.*

At the same time that my father was expressing doubts about what we were attempting, Stalin's work camps were filling with people like us, who would exist the rest of their lives in the darkness and cold of Siberia's long winters, without seeing or hearing from families and friends of their former lives. Many died of hunger and disease.

We had relatives who had been sent to the mouth of the Black Dragon on the east coast, and were never heard from again. Recently, researchers have discovered a railroad tunnel, partially dug under the Tatar Strait, to link the Soviet mainland and Sakhalin Island. When Stalin died, the project stopped, and was never finished, relieving work camp prisoners of the arduous task of completing it.

Papa concluded his journal entry,

> *And yet, we are all now together, safe and healthy. All has gone well so far. Our great God has been with us, and is here now, showering His kindness upon us.*

He and Jakob made it safely back across the river with more of our belongings and money that he had left with Heinrich on his first trip.

We children ran around playing games and being mischievous, but the adults were not used to living crowded together in one small space with children everywhere and nothing to do. As my father put it:

> *One does little else but eat and sleep and stand by the stove. I often think of Abram, an acquaintance back in Russia. How comfortable he was, doing no work all day, his wife running around the village begging for food, while I worked hard providing for my family. So the thoughts travel back and forth from Siberia to Manchuria, always back and forth. It is good, that I do not have to pay for the trips that are in my thoughts; I would be without money already.*

To add to our misery, there were lice in our bedclothes, and bedbugs, as well as cockroaches; and I remember how my mother washed and washed, endlessly trying to get rid of them. We always had to stay hidden under our roof of hay. As my father wrote in his journal:

> *We are living on this farm like ghosts. If my brothers and sisters could see how we live, they would be shocked. But when one is on a journey, one must accommodate one's self to everything. It is simple, but we survive.*

On December 11th, Papa went to meet Aunt Anna Schmidt and our cousins, who were brought across the river on foot by Heinrich. Fortunately, they had been unobserved by any soldier. Papa helped by carrying our youngest cousins. Aunt Anna arrived quite stiff from having climbed up the mountain and down again so fast. Uncle Abe, who had to come separately so as not to be seen with them, was staying in Kotolashka, hidden. He soon, safely followed.

We received letters that had come from America by way of Heinrich. They were from Johan Gossen in answer to Papa's letters, written the past summer. In the letters, he told us we would be able to go to America, news which gave us new hope.

On December 19, Heinrich, who had a Chinese passport, and could speak Chinese, went with Papa and our Manchurian host, on a three-day trip to the village of Katchuriga for documents that would allow us to travel in China. Then, Heinrich and our host went by car to Sachaljan for permission for us to enter Harbin, China, our next stop on our journey. When they came back, Papa took another trip back to Russia to get 1,000 rubles, which he had hidden at Heinrich's house. On his way there, he was taken by Russian soldiers, held several days and questioned, but finally released. He got the money from Heinrich's house, and then came riding back to us on his white horse. What a joy we all felt,when we saw that white horse bringing Papa back to us. We now had 1,000 rubles with us, with another 500 still at Heinrich's house. Father then sold the white horse for 65 rubles in Chinese money, which would have been 130 rubles in Russian money. Papa wrote in his journal:

> *I had hoped the Russian exchange would be better. Last year after the New Year, the Russian money exchange was higher. Hopefully, it will be so this year, also.*

Our cousin Jakob Wiebe, Heinrich and his brother, the Schmidt family, and ours, were now all living with Henry's sister's family. My father wrote:

> *Together we are 18 souls. It is full like a beehive, and what a noise! But we hope always for a different life.*

Papa sold some leather for his brother, Isaak, and thus got some Chinese money, as it was difficult to buy food from the farmers with our Russian money.

On December 24, Uncle Abe and Papa were on their way to the store, when our Manchurian host and Heinrich came back with our documents permitting our entrance into Harbin, China. Heinrich also brought with him the rumor he'd heard that Isaak had been arrested by Communist soldiers. We prayed for Isaak and his family, that they would somehow make it across the border and be able to join us. The men took the papers, and drove to Eigu, where they had to wait three days to have their papers okayed. Then they drove to Zagalon, where they were able to change their money. My father had hoped the exchange would be better. For one Russian ruble, he got only 40 to 50 kopecks in Chinese money. Our family had altogether, $5,500, worth half that much on the exchange. Some in our group had nothing, or very little, because they had had no chance to sell anything before they left. So all the families pooled their money for the trip to Harbin.

Chapter 8

Immigration For Russian Citizens Is Closed

Finally, we could go on to Harbin. We again took the car and drove to Trebek, then took a bus, which was unheated, to Tsitsihar through the Lesser Khingan Mountains. Bandits were known to hold up buses, so Lena and I kept our eyes open watching for them to come riding out of the rocky crevices. Another danger was that buses sometimes broke down, and there was no help available in such a remote area. The women worried about the cold and dangers of the trip through the mountains, so Papa read from Isaiah 49:10-13 for our daily devotions:

> *On every roadway they will graze , and each bare height shall be their pasture. They will never hunger or thirst, scorching wind and sun shall never plague them; for he who pities them will lead them and guide them to springs of water. I will make a highway of all the mountains, and the high roads shall be banked up.* (Jerusalem Bible)

Years later, Mother told us of one bus that did break down. A woman passenger on that bus was expecting a baby that was long overdue. One of the men on a passing bus volunteered to give her his seat, and wait with the broken down bus until help came. She made it safely to Harbin just before her baby arrived, the child being born a month late. From Tsitsihar, we took the train to Harbin, and arrived on December 29, 1928.

In Harbin, we saw the familiar onion-shaped cupolas and spires of Russian churches, and people in brightly colored clothing mingled with the Chinese in their dark clothes of blue and black. We also heard a number of people speaking Russian. Papa told us that Harbin was a city built by Russians as a starting point for the Trans-Siberian Railroad, and the city had many Russian buildings and people. We felt more at home there than we had on the Manchurian farm where we heard only Chinese.

We found a house we could rent, with one room besides the kitchen, for the fifteen of us, while we waited until we could complete our journey.

On January 1, we received a telegram from the border that Uncle Isaak, Aunt Helen, and Jacob Warkentin had made it safely across the border; so we celebrated not only New Year's Day, but a belated Christmas, and the freedom of Isaak and his family. Our group of families pooled our money to send a telegram to our relatives in Canada, telling them of our safe arrival in China. Santa Claus came in spite of our difficult time, bringing fruit and sugar candy, and although there was no fiddle for dancing, we sang. Papa had brought songs with him out of Russia because he had worried that he would no longer have our music in a new land. He had written some of his songs, too, and also a poem:

Praise and glory to the Lord
that He has led us all so well.
No enemy has seen us.
The scales were weighed toward peace.
Yes, the Lord has led us, this we believe.
We lived with enemies,
were looked upon from all sides
as though they would devour us.

Now we live in peace and quiet
and think about what
we've left behind us.

Papa said at the end of our celebration, "We are all alive and safe, and free from the fear of Russian soldiers. The terrors of life in the past are over. That is the greatest gift we could receive this Christmas. Let us give thanks to God for that."

Our Russian worries were over, but we were to find difficulties in China, as well. The two-room house we lived in was so damp the curtains stuck to the windows. We cooked on a small stove (*Karpenski*) that Papa bought, and it worked very well. We ate rice, milk, and bread we bought from the bakery and a few vegetables. The rice was softened in a bucket in the corner, and ladled out and eaten straight from the bucket, uncooked.

One day, I was ladling out some rice while Lena waited for her turn impatiently. I was being maddeningly slow because I had not forgiven her for an unjust punishment.

"Hurry up!" she complained.

I taunted back, "Ladles remind me of a broken window back in Russia, that I got blamed for. When are you going to tell Papa that you threw the ladle at me, and not the other way around?"

"Forget it," she snapped. "He believed me, didn't he?" Years later, when all my brothers and sisters were together for Christmas, we made Lena admit that she had broken the window in trying to hit me with the ladle. Unfortunately, our father was no longer there to learn the truth, and join in our laughter.

In Harbin, we were plagued with lice. We had just one other bucket that had to serve as our water bucket, wash bucket, and even our toilet.

"It's not enough," complained my mother, "for us to have to wash everything constantly, to rid our things of lice. There's also the continuous scrubbing to keep that one bucket sanitary."

Our family had planned that from Harbin, we would go to Canada or the United States. We had already received a letter from Johan Gossen telling us names of offices in Harbin that helped immigrants wanting to go to Canada and the United States. Since Papa and Mama had sisters who had gone to Canada with their families in 1926, it seemed desirable to emmigrate to Canada. One morning while cleaning up the kitchen after breakfast, Lena and I heard the adults in the other room speaking in serious voices. Uncle Abe's voice stood out clearly above the rest.

"Immigration for Russian citizens is now closed to Canada and the United States. The government quotas have been filled." There was stunned silence.

"There are 215 of us Mennonites now in Harbin, working to find lands where we can be safe from persecution," Papa added.

"We could go to Paraguay and join my sister and her family there," suggested my mother.

"But it is wild and unsettled, and we would have to clear the land and begin life as pioneers, as our ancestors did in Russia years ago. With our growing families, we have enough work to do without the hardships the Paraguayan pioneers are facing," my father countered.

In a letter my father had written in 1926 to our relatives in Canada, he told how he had just finished building us a new house and barn, and how pleased he was with it. He had bought a new threshing machine and some new land that did not need plowing. I could understand how hard it was for him to leave what we had, and the heartbreak of having to start all over in a wilderness area.

“Our only choice,” offered my uncle, “is to become Chinese citizens and immigrate to the United States under the still open quota for Chinese. We will need to live in China at least nine months before we can become Chinese citizens.” That is what our small band of Mennonites decided to do. They ended their meeting by singing one of the hymns Papa had brought with him from Russia.

And so it was that the fifteen of us in the little Chinese house in Harbin would need to survive there for at least nine months. Once again on our journey, we felt kin to Noah as we tried to cope with close quarters. As least we had no animals to take care of.

We did soon have another person on board our ark. The old Chinese lady who had predicted back at the farm that my mother’s unborn child would not live was proven wrong, for on February 1, 1929, my sister Elsa was born, a healthy baby who was to be the strongest child of us all, even to this day; and she was already a Chinese citizen!

A Chinese midwife was called for, as was the custom, but when she arrived, she was so dirty, my father showed her the door, saying, “I’ll do it myself!” and with the assistance of my sister, Lena, he delivered the baby, himself. I watched and remembered, and the experience was to be a help in later life, when I, too, would assist in delivering babies.

Aron Warkentin in the Medical Corps in Siberia

Chapter 9

You Must Bind Her Feet!

Elsa arrived in the midst of the Chinese New Year celebration of the year 4626. Skies sparkled with fireworks and blazed with red banners. Musicians and long dragons whose legs were dancers, wound their way through the streets of Harbin to strange oriental music. Ice sculptures glowed in colored lights along the Songhua River, a tributary of the Black Dragon. Street vendors were coaxing us to take home a live snake in honor of the Year of the Snake. My mother shuddered, but we children would have been delighted to have a pet snake.

The festive occasion matched our joy at having a healthy baby in our home. The old year had been the Year of the Dragon, and the Black Dragon had not swallowed us, or harmed our little sister, as our mother had crossed its icy waters. Papa told us that our trip across had been three miles long, and we praised God we had all made it unharmed.

We were a curiosity to our Chinese neighbors, and the birth of a child in our household brought the ladies in to visit, and offer small gifts. Just as all babies cry in the same language, women the world over rejoice in the arrival of a new baby, and desire to hold the child, and marvel at the tiny fingers and toes. Most of them showed sympathetic faces when they learned the baby was not male, while Lena and I were delighted to finally have a baby sister after two bothersome boys. One elderly woman was particularly agitated, and kept pointing to Elsa's bare and kicking feet. Another visitor, a Mennonite lady who had been in Harbin a while, translated her words for us, "She says you must bind her feet! Otherwise, they will not be small and beautiful when she grows up."

Fortunately, my parents would have none of that in our family. I learned later that back then, the girl baby's feet were not just tightly bound. The arch was broken first and then the foot bound. The purpose was not just for beauty of the small feet and dainty steps, but also to restrict women so they could not move about freely and possibly become involved with undesirable people. It is now an illegal procedure in China. My parents certainly did not want to restrict our ability to move around, be helpful, and do our share of the work. Nor did they want to restrict our freedom. Our family had had enough of that!

Elsa was so tiny and pretty, like a little doll, that I no longer cared that I had left my doll back in Russia. Now I had a real live baby to help care for, and this time I was old enough to be of some help.

I remember another time my father helped my mother with a medical problem. After the baby was born, she had developed a painful cyst in her breast. My father took a knife, sterilized it, and used vinegar to sterilize her skin. He then cut a star shape in her breast and pushed out the cyst. For my father, delivering babies and removing cysts were not unusual tasks, as he had been in the medical corps back in Siberia.

Our mother told us, "When Lena was born, your father was away serving in the Russian medical corps, and for ten months I did not know whether he was dead or alive. He had been inducted as part of the agreement with Nicholas Romanov when he opened southeastern Siberia and offered it to Mennonites for settlement. Each of our families was given 150 acres of land and $550 for expenses, and promised no interference in Mennonite education or civil affairs. We were given immunity from serving in the army, due to our religious belief against killing for any reason, but our men would be expected to serve in the forestry or medical corps. Shortly after Lena was born, I was preparing to move back to my parents' home," my mother continued, "when Papa returned, dragged on a sled by horses. He was very ill with typhoid fever, and I nursed him until he finally recovered."

"Where had the family lived before moving to Siberia?" I asked.

"Your father and I were both born in Holland to German Mennonite parents. Due to religious persecution, our families moved to the Kuban River area in southwestern Russia near the Black Sea. It was 1900, when I was only 8 months old. Later, the czar opened land to be settled in Siberia. Your grandfather was a doctor, a bone specialist, and was needed there, as people were often snowed in due to heavy storms. We lived in a Mennonite community of five villages, and were happy and prosperous, until persecution once again began when Nicholas was killed, and civil war was going on in Russia. The White Army and the Red Army fought each other for power, with Lenin leading the Red, or Communist Army, and Kerensky, the White. The Red Army under Lenin took control.

"In World War I, Russia fought Germany under Lenin and people in Russia were forbidden to speak German, and were persecuted for any connection with Germany. Then Stalin came to power, and established Gulag, a system of work camps for all enemies of Communism. Once again our family now is moving to find a new land in which to be free to live, and worship God in our own way."

Soon after we had arrived in Harbin, my father began making plans.

"Neta," he said one day as snow fell down across our window, "I must get a job, if we are to be here in China for a while. In Russia, I learned to drive a tractor. I can just as easily learn to drive a car. Perhaps I can be a chauffeur, or an engineer on the trains." He began taking a course to be an engineer. He also found a bike and learned to ride it, so our family had a way, besides walking, to get around in the city.

The snow had disappeared, and trees were showing signs of spring when my father found the American consulate. With the help of his bike, he had become familiar with the streets of Harbin, in spite of his inability to speak or read Chinese. Through the consulate, he met a Mennonite doctor, John Isaac, an opthamologist who had left Russia before the Russian revolution. Dr. Isaac had gone to college with Reverend Regere, who was a minister in a large Mennonite church in Reedley, California. The doctor said he would write to Reverend Regere and tell him we wanted to get into the United States and needed a sponsor. Dr. Isaac also told Papa, "Gather together as many Mennonites in Harbin as you can locate. Form a group and petition the American government to allow you to enter their country and settle there."

My father came home that day with renewed hope. He wrote in his journal:

> *"When Jesus got out of the boat, he saw the large crowd, and took pity on them. They were like sheep without a shepherd" (Mark 6:34). No longer sheep without a shepherd, we now have the guidance of Dr. Isaac, to continue our journey.*

For guidance, there would continue to be shepherds provided along the way, as well as the Bible my father had brought out of Russia hidden under his coat.

Also, Dr. Isaac warned my father that we should have physical examinations, because no country would let us immigrate if we were not well. He agreed to give us health examinations. I remember him flipping back my eyelids with his fingers, peering into my eyes, and saying: "She has tracoma." My mother had it, also. It explained why she had lately been holding onto Papa's jacket to let him guide her when they went somewhere. Our eyesight had been gradually becoming clouded, to the extent that we could not see very well to do ordinary tasks. Tracoma was a highly contagious eye disease common among immigrants of European extraction, but rare in the United States. It seemed strange that Mama and I were the only ones in our famiy to have the disease considering the close quarters we had been living in since we had started out on our journey out of Russia. It would take six months of treatment before we could be cured and allowed to enter another country. Treatment and medication were needed and turned out to be expensive, but by the following July, we were cured.

Dr. Isaac had suggested the name of a tutor who could begin to teach us all English while we waited out our stay in China. What a blessing our shepherd/doctor turned out to be!

The day came when Uncle Isaak, Aunt Helen, and their four children joined us in Harbin. Like my father previously, Isaak had been taken by Communist soldiers near the Russian border, kept a few days, and then released. Heinrich Michelson then took him across the Amur River to join his wife and children previously hidden at the same farm where we had been hidden. In Harbin, they were able to rent a room across the street from us. There were now 84 of us Mennonites in Harbin who had crossed the border from Russia into China after leaving our Slavgorad-Reinfeld area. Heinrich Michelson; his wife, Katherine; daughter, Lydia, 2; and their baby, Katherine, born just one week before leaving Russia, had come to Harbin, also. Another Elsa had been born, too, the first girl for Uncle Abram and Aunt Anna. Lena and I were glad to see the number of girls gaining on the number of boys in our group.

Following Dr. John Isaac's advice, Papa got the community of 215 Mennonites in Harbin organized. They met at the

Russian Baptist Church in Harbin, where a number of men formed a committee. John Frieson was chosen to compose a letter in Russian, to be translated later into English. It was to be sent to the newly inaugurated President of the United States, Herbert Hoover. In his letter, he stated the details of our recent escape from Communist persecution, and our desire for a new homeland of freedom. He added at the end, " The Mennonites are frugal, industrious farmers who will be a credit to the United States." One of the farmers had a photograph of his prosperous farm, and suggested it be included with the letter to show the success of Mennonite farmers in Russia.

M. B. Fast, who had been one of the Americans who had brought free food to our settlements in Russia during the famine of 1919, also pleaded our cause in Washington, D.C., as did Fridtjof Nansen, the Arctic explorer and humanitarian.

The answer from the U.S. government was:

> *The Mennonites will be allowed to come, a few at a time, 15 per month.You must pay your way and be physically able. No handicapped people will be allowed.*

A problem of many now was that they no longer had money. They had spent it all getting to Harbin. A way would have to be found to finance the crossing. Uncle Isaak had found a good job in a German athletic club, but German language jobs were not easy to find.

I had sometimes watched the wealthy people play tennis where Uncle Isaak worked, and knew they paid people to collect their tennis balls for them.

"Lena," I suggested one day, "why don't we try to get a job gathering tennis balls at the German Club? We could do that. It has to be easier that sitting in that crowded room listening to relatives complain. It has to be easier than gathering eggs as we used to on the farm!"

"We'd have to get Father's permission, and he'd never give it," she asserted.

"You ask him," I begged. "He listens to you." It always seemed to me that Lena had more influence on Papa than the rest of us. She was the oldest, but she also was good at picking up languages. He took her with him sometimes to translate Chinese for him, as she had already learned a number of phrases in the language.

"Papa," she began the next day, "we need money for our trip to the United States, don't we?"

"Yes," he agreed.

"Well, we've seen rich people pay children to collect their tennis balls at the German Club where Uncle Isaak works. Could we do that, too? We'd stay together and watch out for each other." Lena had a way of knowing what Papa was thinking. "It would be good exercise for us and a chance to be outdoors. We're so cooped up all day!"

From Uncle Isaak we learned they were looking for children who were quick on their feet. Many of the Chinese girls had had their feet bound as babies and could not move as fast as we could. Chinese boys could get better paying jobs elsewhere.

Papa at first was doubtful, but finally agreed, saying, "I will walk you to work and return for you at the end of the day." He explained in detail how to behave in the city around men, and the danger of us being out alone without an escort.

"Make no eye contact nor show any familiarity with the Chinese people. Wait at the tennis court until I come."

But one day, he was held up at a meeting, and came later than usual. Some men came after us, and one pursuer had dragged Lena into the ditch along the side of the road. My father arrived in time to chase the men off before any harm had come to us. It was hard to believe that ordinary people who had passed by and seen us in danger had done nothing to help us. After that, we waited for Papa inside Uncle Isaak's office, where we were away from danger.

On July 29, Papa wrote in a letter to my aunt in Canada:

> *We get no letters from Russia here, as both sides of the border are closed, and it looks like war is coming. Communists from Russia wanted to overthrow the government in China, but it didn't work. Instead, they are being sent out of Harbin, about 100 a day. It is really something for us to see. It smelled like Communism, but now they are sent back. I was at the railroad station and watched all this. The guards treated them like dogs, even whipped them. The women and children were crying because they wanted to stay in Harbin. It really was quite a sad sight.*

Committee formed at Harbin, China, to find a place and a way to emigrate. Papa is in the back row, first on the left.

Chapter 10

The Town Is Full Of Mennonites!

Although Harbin was a large, international city, it was difficult for adults to find work. Finally, two Mennonites who had enough money to pay for tickets, volunteered to go to Reedley, California, to seek financial help from the Mennonite Cental Committee that had helped the Russian Mennonites during the Famine of 1919. Dr. Isaac's brother, James Isaac, and John Friesson, eventually sent us news of their trip:

> *When we arrived in the United States, we bought a car. James had a Harbin license, having driven his brother's car in Harbin, and I had the money to pay for the car. In Reedley, we drove up and down Rt. 99 looking for Mennonites, by knocking on doors, and asking, "Mennonites? Mennonites?" To our surprise, we usually were answered in German and discovered that the town was full of Mennonites.*
>
> *"We are looking for Mr. and Mrs. Weins, retired missionaries we were told could help us."*
>
> *We were soon given directions to find Mrs. Weins. Her husband is now deceased.*
>
> *"Yes, yes," she said, "we have been expecting you. You can stay in my house while you are here. We want you to come to our church and tell everyone of the plight of the Mennonites in China. Many of us came through what you are now facing, and you will surely be helped!"*

At the Mennonite Brethren Church, we gave a talk telling all of our experiences in our recent escape from Russian Communists.

"You will receive all the help from us that we can possibly give, but you must also go to Kansas City where the Mennonite Central Committee will soon be holding a conference. Tell your story there to the Immigration Council. They are the national group who helped Russian Mennonites during the famine of 1919."

We were accompanied by several members of the Mennonite Brethren Church and traveled to Kansas City to make our presentation, telling of our permission from the United States to immigrate. We told of our need for financial help, and that we would expect to pay back all that we were loaned. After consideration, the Immigration Committee announced that $140 would be given to each person toward passage, and $10 to each for expenses. The money was to be paid back when each family was settled and able to do so.

After this report from the two men who had represented us in the United States, the group in our small house celebrated with prayers and songs of thanks and much discussion about the anticipated new life in the United States.

It was at this time that we received from the Canadian German Council the news that we could get German passports without permission from the Russian or Chinese govenments to go to Canada. We decided that if we could go to Canada sooner than the United States, we would do so, as the longer we stayed in China, the less money we had.

Soon after that, however, we learned from the United States that our family had been chosen to be in the first group of Mennonites to leave Harbin, so we decided to go to the

United States instead of Canada. We had been in China nine months and were, therefore, able to become citizens of China and obtain Chinese passports, in order to enter the United States as Chinese citizens.

But passports cost $25 per person and entry fees $36. When Papa totaled our money, we heard his cry of dismay, "Neta, we are short money for passage in spite of the amount promised from the Reedley Mennonites. What shall we do? It is unthinkable to leave anyone behind in China!"

Back in Russia, while we were still on our farm in Slavgorad, Papa's sister and her husband had emigrated to Canada with their children. Due to lack of enough money for passage on the ship, their eldest son, Heinrich, had been left on the dock at the seaport, Sagradowka, as the rest of them sailed for Canada. Money from the sale of their farm and auction of their things after they left, was sent to Heinrich in Sagradowka. It was a sum better than hoped for. Eventually, Heinrich received the money and made it to Canada by freighter. He then hitchhiked to Van Couver and bought land across from his father's farm, but he never forgave his father for leaving him. When his father was dying of a heart attack, he let him lie, and did nothing to get him help.

"Well," my mother replied, "if the girls were each two years younger, we would have enough money. Of course, we cannot lie."

"And break a Commandment? I cannot do that!"

"But remember the ox down the well on the Sabbath? The Bible says you should save it, does it not?" my mother queried slyly. "Remember the time you lied to the Communist soldiers to save our lives?" My mother won that argument. Nevertheless, they prayed about it for several days.

"I must do this which I do not believe in doing, for the sake of our family," my father sighed, giving in; but he never got over having to break a Commandment for any reason.

He explained to Lena and me what he was going to do and why. "Neta, you are now 8 instead of 10, and Lena, you are 9 instead of 11." He then applied for our passports, and the day came when he announced to us, "All documents are made out for landing in San Francisco, and we have tickets for sailing on October 11, 1929. We are ready to go!"

My aunt and uncle and cousins, who were living with us, would not be leaving at the same time, so our celebration party was also a good-bye party. Our families would be separating, at least for the time being. Our celebration however, was premature. Ten days before leaving, my father received a telegram.

"It is from a Mr. Krehbiel in Washington," he said. "He sends us money, but says we are to go to Seattle, not San Francisco. Do you remember that we recently sent a man named John Friessen ahead to represent us in Reedley, California?" My mother nodded. "Well, he wrote to Mr. Krehbiel that the Mennonites decided all United Church members were to go to Seattle, and the Mennonite Brethren were to go to San Francisco." We were United Church members.

"What can we do now?" moaned my mother. "I knew something would go wrong!"

"We will pray," was his answer, "and we will telegram back that we have already made reservations and bought tickets for San Francisco. Surely God has not brought us this far only to abandon us now."

Mr. Krehbiel's reply to my father's telegram was:

> *Come ahead, but be prepared to go on to Seattle by land when you arrive. The Mennonites have set things up that way, and I have told them you will comply with their arrangements so as not to complicate matters.*

The money sent to us from the Mennonites was a loan. Since we had only $40 left after buying our tickets to San Francisco, our relatives would be traveling directly to Seattle, since they had not yet bought their tickets, or made any arrangements to leave China.

I think of what my father wrote to his sister in Canada. His letter that she sent us recently, is like his voice from the past. He wrote her,

> *Since coming to China, I have learned to drive an auto, ride a bike, and engineer a train. I've learned, also, that you should cherish your home and homeland, if you have them.*

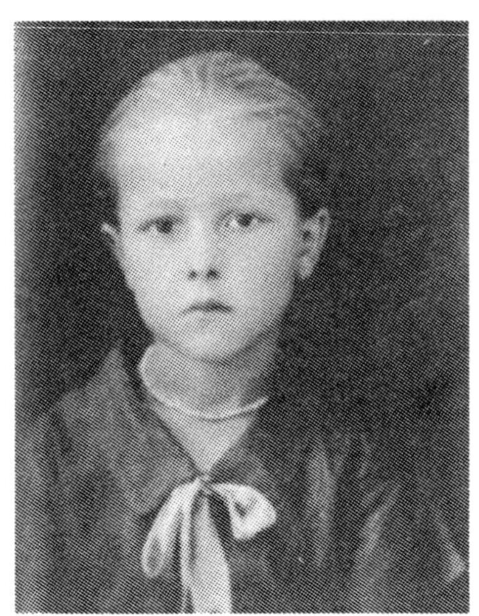

Me

Papa, Jake, Johan, Lena, and me

Chapter 11

Where Will The Last Resting Place Be?

We parted with our aunts, uncles, and cousins, not knowing if we'd even make it safely across the Pacific Ocean. At our parting, Uncle Abe recited a poem for us that he had written:

Where will be the last resting place
for a tired wanderer?
Will it be under the palms in the South?
or the linden trees on the Rhine?
Or will I be buried by the hand
of a stranger in the desert?
Or will I rest by the seashore in the sand?
At any rate, God's heaven will surround me,
Instead of glowing candles,
the stars shall shine for me.
— Abram Schmidt, Sept. 16, 1929

We took a train from Harbin to Korea, across Korea to the ocean, and then a ferry from Korea to Yokohama, Japan, where we stayed several weeks with a Japanese family until our ship was ready to leave. I liked the Japanese family and wouldn't have minded staying longer, but on October 11, our ship, the *S. Asoma Maru*, sailed out of Yokohama Bay for San Francisco. It was a Japanese cargo ship, and Lena and I had watched on the deck as the crew had loaded cargo into the ship with ropes and pulley and lowered it into the hold.

Our journey started calmly, the ship rocking gently on sun-glazed water. Once out beyond sight of Japan, our view was endless sky and endless sea in all directions, even underneath, where creatures swam. We strained to see some evidence of whales or fish, but only gulls, eager for bits of food, followed behind our ship.

"This must be what the world looked like to Noah," Lena exclaimed to me in awe.

There were shouts of the crew, calling to one another in Japanese, and bells marking the days' divisions. Children were running about as mischievous as on shore; nothing ever seemed to keep our little brothers from their play!

Officers in their gold buttoned white suits sauntered through the hallways, and sweaty sailors handling ropes and heavy equipment scurried around on deck. The air was warm and humid, and our cheeks stung with salt mist, as did our lips and tongues when we opened our mouths to speak.

We became used to the engines' steady humming and the sudden lurches of the ship as we lay on our cots at night and slipped into dreams of a land where we would be safe and free.

One night, I was wakened from such a dream by the sound of sliding furniture, people talking, and children crying. As I became fully awake, I was aware the ship was tossing violently, and I was filled with a nauseous feeling of dizziness.

"Lena," I called across the dark to her, "I don't feel so well."

"Neither do I," she groaned. "We're in a storm, and I think we're seasick." The rest of the family was fine.

That night marked the beginning of a seige of seasickness that held us captive for the greater part of our ocean trip. We spent those days in the hold, while upstairs, there were people to meet, and food to enjoy, but we could not eat. We were given pickles to suck on that helped settle our stomachs, but we ate little else.

While on the ship, we met a pretty woman who was very friendly toward us. One of our fellow Mennonites warned us, "I'm suspicious of her. We are strangers to her and she is unnaturally friendly. Don't pay any attention to her."

On October 16, five days into our trip across the ocean, we did not count one day, so we had two October 16ths in order to be with American time. Our ship landed at the Hawaiian Islands to deliver supplies, and Lena and I had a respite from our seasickness. Then the ship sailed on, and our inability to eat returned.

At last, our ship approached Angel Island across the bay from San Francisco. It was October 25, 1929; and four days later, in New York City, the Stock Market crashed, and the United States was plunged into economic depression.

We were taken from the ship in a small boat, and custom officers met us at the dock. As my brother, Jake remembered, "We were all happy, and scared to death, dressed in our Sunday clothes, and ready with the required papers."

The women and children were separated from the men, and Mama was very upset. Leaving Russia had meant to her she would no longer have to be separated from my father. "You know what government officials were like in Russia! How can we trust government officials here in a strange land where we can't even understand what they say?" My father's reply was, "We can trust God. He has led us so far. He will not let us down now." In his pocket, he had $40 left of the $5,500 we had taken with us from Russia.

The reason for the separation was that everyone had to take off all his clothes and have his body and clothes checked for contraband. We learned later that the lady who had tried to make friends with us on the ship had been caught trying to put smuggled diamonds into luggage of immigrating families because their luggage was less likely to be searched.

We were given steel mesh cots in a dormitory room, the walls covered with Chinese poems that displayed the anger and sorrow of immigrants who had come without the necessary papers, and were being held until their documents could be obtained.

To Lena and me, the food we were given was delicious after our long ocean fast. There was also a playground with swings, slides, and merry-go-round and we children began to relax a little, playing on equipment we had never seen before.

We were to stay on Angel Island for 21 days, to be thoroughly checked before being allowed to enter the United States. We had to undergo examination of our bodies, head to toe, bowels, urine, and all.

"We will be sent back to China if we do not pass their examination," explained Lena. "We are still Chinese citizens."

"Imagine if it was you or I that had to be sent back, or Jake, or Johan, or our baby sister, Elsa!" I worried.

One child we knew of had not been allowed to enter at Seattle because inspectors had discovered he had once had polio. It was not known at that time whether polio was contagious, so he was sent back to China. His parents went on without him.

We also had to undergo questioning. Each member of our family except Johan and Elsa, was taken alone into a room, and asked questions to find out information about our past, and what our future ambitions were. Mother and Father were asked many other questions, also.

"Age? Sex? Marital status, occupation, literacy, nationality, last residence, final destination, how our journey was financed, how much money we had now, and who would meet us. Had we ever been in the United States before? Had we ever been in prison? In an almshouse? Had we ever received charity? Were we polygamists? Were we in the United States for contract labor? Were any of us deformed or crippled?"

The questions seemed endless, but we passed. Thanks to Dr. Isaac in China, we also passed our health examinations.

We were finally cleared to go ashore. That evening Papa announced it to us, he read from his Bible, Psalm 124:

If it had not been the Lord who was on our side,
let Israel now say —
if it had not been the Lord
who was on our side,
when men rose up against us,
then they would have swallowed us up alive,
when their anger was kindled against us;
then the flood would have swept us away,
the torrent would have gone over us;
then over us would have gone the raging waters.
Blessed be the Lord,
who has not given us as prey to their teeth!
We have escaped as a bird
from the snare of the fowlers;
the snare is broken,
and we have escaped!
Our help is in the name of he Lord,
who made heaven and earth. (RSV)

Papa wrote to his sister in Canada later, "The travel from China to California was good, it was lovely weather, we saw much. In all, it was 2,870 miles." He forgot to tell her about the rough sea, and our seasickness!

At my Uncle Abe's grave showing the poem he wrote.

Chapter 12

Every Man 'neath His Vine And Fig Tree ...

At last we were transported in a small boat across the bay to the mainland. When we stepped onto American soil, Papa shouted, "Alleluia!" and kissed Mama. We all hugged and cheered.

The United States government helped us put our past behind us, for as we entered their country, they changed my name to Agnes, and my mother's name to Agnes Neta. Lena, whose name was Helena, became Helen, Johan became John, and Elsa became Alice. Papa and Jake's names remained the same except they spelled Jakob's name, Jacob. Lena and I needed to remember that our ages had been altered in China, and we were entering two years younger.

We were met on the dock by members of the Reedley Mennonite Brethren Church and taken by bus to Reedley, California, a small town near Fresno, where the minister, Reverend Regere, welcomed us cordially, in spite of the early hour of 4 a.m. We were grateful to be taken to a house of our own, in a Mennonite complex, like a labor camp, where we already had jobs set up for us, working in the fields. The house was small, but compared to our two rooms in China, it was wonderful; and there would be just our family living there. A huge fig tree stood outside the house and shaded the yard, and in the background, we could see the vineyards of grapes, where we would soon be picking and earning a living.

Our new home had a stove and furniture, and was supplied with food, clothes, baby things, even live chickens! The people of the church had prepared a meal for us, and Papa said to them, "Thank you for all you have provided for us and for giving us such a welcome. Best of all, we are surrounded by people who love God, and care for us, people who know what we have been through, since you, too, came out of the same persecution, to this land of freedom."

"Look how much like us they are!" I said to Helen. "So much blond hair and blue eyes; and we can understand what they say! It's like being home again...."

"And even their clothes are similar," Helen finished for me. We were to make new friends quickly, as we all had the same background.

The next morning, our neighbors brought breakfast completely prepared. We never stopped marveling at God's blessings showered upon us.

But in America, there were differences, just as there had been in China, new things to see and learn. We had no experience with Halloween, and thought it a strange custom. We had never tasted peaches, and thought they were wonderful. My mother thought shredded wheat cereal, odd, "Like eating hay," she commented, and Helen complained, "The beds are too soft and make me seasick! I'll sleep on the floor." I was happy to have a whole bed to myself, for a while, anyway.

Helen and I began school, finding it difficult, at first, because of our language. My father helped us learn more quickly by forbidding us to speak German in our home.

"This is our country, now," he said, "and we will show our respect by learning to speak its language. From now on, in this household, only English will be spoken. Everything that Helen and Agnes learn in school during the day, they will teach the rest of us when they come home."

At first, we were constantly slipping back into German before we realized it, but Helen picked up the new language easily, and my laughter at our mistakes helped relieve the tension when we took it too seriously. We were beginning to relax and lose our fear and worry now that our long journey was over.

But Papa had not forgotten that we were to travel on to Seattle, to settle with the others of the United Mennonite Church who had come from China. He made inquiries, and soon Mr. Krehbiel arrived and provided us with a car to drive to Seattle. After some experience with it, however, Papa decided it would be difficult in wintertime to drive the seven of us to Seattle in that one small car. So it was decided that we would remain in California, at least for the time being.

California was beautiful, although winters were wetter than we were used to, sometimes too wet. But the land in spring was covered with poppies, lupines, buttercups, and Indian paintbrush, yellow mustard, and violets. Horses ran wild in the hills, and rivers flowed deeply, gorged with winter rains. But in summer, the rivers went underground, and the rain was replaced with hot wind and dust. Irrigation was necessary then. But the land was deep with rich soil and the farming was good. With the flowers and sunshine, and warm climate, we girls felt like the forty-niners we heard about in school, only the rich soil was our gold.

We all picked grapes, oranges, olives, and even watermelons. Babies were put on blankets in the shade while their mothers picked. I can still see my mother, once again pregnant, sitting high on a melon truck, catching the enormous watermelons that we children tossed up to her. How she caught them without a lap, I'll never know.

When there was no fruit to pick, Papa got a job making hay. The farmer gave him a team of mules, a Jack and a Jennie, to work the fields. Dad would take Jake along to watch from under a shady tree while he worked. As Jake tells it:

> *Dad would mow the hay, wait a day or two depending on the weather, and then put the mules on*

a hay rake that rolled the hay up in itself. Every so often, Dad would kick a lever and the rake would open and leave the hay. When the mules needed a water break, Dad would come over and talk with me, explaining to me how the machine worked. He explained how a drive wheel turned a gear that made the mowing bar go up, and when it got so high, it automatically dropped down.

One day, Dad was raking with the mules, and a horsefly or something, bit one of them. The mules took off running while the rake was up, and as it automatically dropped down, Dad fell forward and under the rake. He was dragged quite a long way, and his head was cut open.

I ran for Mom, who brought Dad's medical kit. She cleaned his head, and since Dad would not go to a doctor, she used his medication to sterilize the opening, and then sewed it up with needle and thread, just as Dad had done in Russia while in the medical corps. In those days, you didn't have pain killers. If you got hurt, you had pain. It was expected.

Someone caught the mules and brought them back to the barn. Dad healed in time.

My father missed the kind of farming he was used to, where irrigating was not necessary, and the climate was cooler. In Siberia, 65 degrees was the high in summer. Winters were a bitter 30 to 40 degrees below 0 at times; but it was a dry cold, and we were used to it.

One day a Dr. Mosiman, from Bluffton College in Bluffton, Ohio, came to California to visit Reverend Regere, who had been minister of the Grace Mennonite Church in Pandora, Ohio, for eight years. Reverend Regere told Dr. Mosiman about my father wanting to farm as he had back in Russia. After Dr. Mosiman returned to Ohio, he sent a letter to my father. Papa came in to dinner one day beaming, and waving the letter.

"Agnes, we have a chance to go to Ohio and farm as we like. Dr. Mosselman has offered me a job with Bluffton College. They've acquired 450 acres near Washington Court House, a small town in central Ohio, and need someone to farm it. They're asking us. They'll even provide us with a house. Look here on this map he sends. It will be cooler there, like home."

Mother looked, noting the long distance between California and Ohio. "Oh, Aron, not another move with five children and another on the way! It will mean crossing an unfamiliar land of mountains and prairies when we've just gotten settled here, among caring people. They've made us feel so welcome. We barely know the language and won't know a soul!"

The Reedley Church had become a support system for our family, and the building itself, a sanctuary in more ways than one. We children had begun to call it "the place where Mama goes to cry." She began to cry now, but Papa was a salesman, and knew the right thing to say.

"We'll write Isaak and Helen, and Abe and Anna in Seattle, and see if they want to go with us. We'll all be together again and the children will be growing up with aunts, uncles, and cousins, as they were before."

Mama finally agreed, but not without quoting Uncle Abe's poem, "Where will be the last resting place...?"

The Schmidts and the Isaak Warkentins had landed in Seattle as we were to have done, and were working in canning factories there. My father wrote them, telling of his plan to move to Ohio where farming would be similar to what our families were used to.

Although our family had decided to move to an area of the United States that was more like our former home in

Siberia, there were often days and nights when part of our past came back to haunt us.

One day, as Papa was cutting the grass out on the edge of the grape vines, Jake, John, and Alice were playing nearby, while Mother, Helen, and I were still picking grapes. As the sun got lower in the late afternoon sky, they started home through the grape vines. As they turned a corner and looked up, something dark loomed ahead, and they were so frightened that Jake picked up Alice, grabbed John's hand, and ran as well as he could, to find Mother.

"There's men out there, and they are coming to get us!" he cried.

"I don't think there's anybody out there," Papa said, coming when he heard the crying. He took Jake by the hand, the rest of us following, and walked back out to where the children had been. At the end of the vineyard was a railroad tie propped against a fence that cast a shadow across the bare field. Then, as Jake retold it later,

> *We all walked back to our home, and while Helen and Agnes lit the kerosene lamps, and Mama made supper, Dad sat with me in his lap, on the front porch of our cabin, and sang to me, "Every man 'neath his vine and fig tree, shall live at peace and unafraid ..."* (Micah 4:14). *The words from that song are taken from the Bible, Jake, but it's talking about us, too. See the fig tree, here, hanging over our house, and the grape vines all around us? We will live at peace and unafraid, just like it says in the Bible, because God has always taken care of us. He will be with us here, too.*
>
> *That evening, after a supper of Mom's wonderful cooking, we laughed and sang together. I went to bed, my brother and sisters sleeping around me, knowing that my parents were in the next room,*

and we were safe in a new world. I no longer needed to worry that anyone was going to knock on the door in the night, and take us away. That fig tree out there reminded me every day.

We received letters from Uncle Abe and Uncle Isaak saying they were all coming. We children were excited. There would be eleven cousins coming. Mother, too, was happy, as she especially missed the company of her sister and sister-in-law.

Our parents had been able to save most of the money earned. Food came from our garden and chickens, and Mother made all our clothes. Gifts were homemade, too. Our father made toys for us from wood, and dolls were sewn by Mother. That past winter in California, Papa had made for Jake and John, a beautiful red wagon using empty spools for wheels.

One day, he took Jake to San Francisco, and they checked out sale lots of used trucks. Finally, he picked out a new, green 1928 Chevrolet truck for $285. After the dealer showed him how to drive it, the two came home, sitting proudly there in the cab, faces beaming. We were to be in Ohio by Thanksgiving for the new job with Bluffton College, and the truck was going to get us there.

Behind the cab was nothing but a flat bed on wheels, so the next day, they set off again, this time for the lumber store, and came back with materials to make us the first "camper" we had ever seen. Papa built a little room behind the truck cab, cutting a window in the cab wall, so Mama could keep an eye on us kids from her seat beside Papa in the cab. The rear wall opened at the middle and folded down, so we kids could see out, and there were double doors on each side, similar to those on modern vans. Papa put a davenport in where we could sit or lie down.

The Schmidts came to California to join us, traveling down the western coast from Seattle to Reedley. The Isaak Warkentins came a week after them. Most of our group of Mennonites who had left Harbin, China, remained in the Seattle area permanently.

Chapter 13

Are We Ever Going To Get There?

Uncle Abe and his family arrived in a Model T touring car, open like a convertible. Our fascination with it equaled our delight in our new truck. The Isaak Warkentin family arrived in their car soon afterward, and as we crossed the country, we kids took turns riding in each of the vehicles with different combinations of relatives.

In October of 1930, we set out for Ohio needing to be there by Thanksgiving for our jobs on two farms owned by Bluffton College.

Food was packed onto the truck, as well as our belongings. There was dried meat, dried fruit, beans, crackers, anything that would not spoil. Gallon water bags hung on the outside of the truck and cars, where it kept cold. We could get fresh water out of creeks and rivers in those days.

Several jugs of water were stored in the truck for use when the radiator overheated. A large cardboard box was packed into the truck to set up around our outdoor "portable pottie" for privacy.

In the evenings, when it was time to stop, we would pull off the road and camp for the night. The men and boys would gather wood and build a fire, while the women, and Helen and I would prepare a meal, and then clean up afterward. The little kids were free to run and play to make up for all the sitting they'd been doing all day.

At night, some slept in the cars, some in the truck, and some in tents improvised from blankets. We didn't have to worry about anyone coming along and hurting us. We kept a stick handy in case a bear or mountain lion came along, but wild animals never bothered us. As Jake, 6 years old at the time, remembed later, "No one will ever know the feeling of freedom we had after our experiences in Communist Russia. We all felt at home because we were in a free country."

I remember our 1928 Chevrolet truck with all of us children piled in the back, taking us right through huge cut out redwood trees in California. Our biggest challenge came soon afterward, as we crossed the mountains. Brakes were not as good as they are today, so Uncle Isaak rode outside our truck, sitting on the fender with a log in his arms. When the truck got too warm going up a mountain, he'd hop off, and place the log behind the back tires to keep it from rolling backward while we waited for the truck to cool. The same was done if we had to stop on our way down a mountain.

When we came to flat country, it was much easier. None of us knew United States geography, or English very well, so when we crossed a state or river, we were not familiar with their names as American citizens would have been. We tried to learn as we went along. We saw mostly wheat and corn fields, farms, and small towns similar to what we'd seen in Russia.

We worked at jobs when we could find them along the way. It was harvest time and there were jobs available where farmers had survived the drought. There was wood to chop, and other outdoor chores people were willing to pay us for.

It was a long, slow ride for a truck full of children. "Are we ever going to get there?" we frequently asked, and Papa responded, "God will get us there."

We didn't dare fight with each other, but whiled away the time playing games and singing, with no fear this time that anyone would overhear us and arrest us for whatever language we chose to sing in.

About two weeks after leaving California, we arrived in Ohio. In the two years since we had left home, we had crossed southeastern Siberia by train, hidden on a Manchurian farm, worked at a tennis court in Harbin, China, stayed with a family in Japan, sailed the Pacific Ocean, picked fruit in California, and crossed western United States on Highway 66 in a truck. As children, we were always "at home" not only because we were free, as Jake remembered, but also because we were with loving parents, brothers and sisters, aunts, uncles, and cousins. Our little community moved with us as we went. It would soon break apart in astounding ways, but for the time being, we were secure, feeling nothing was really changing in our tight group.

When we arrived in northwest Ohio, the leaves had already turned and fallen, and fields lay bare from harvest. We reported to Bluffton College, in the town of Bluffton, and were welcomed by the members of the Ebenezer Mennonite Church. The Schmidts were placed on a farm in Beaverdam, Ohio, near Bluffton, and our family and the Isaak Warkentins were put in an old brick house near them.

"Are we finally at our new farm?" Jake asked, and Mama had to answer, "Not quite, Jake. Our new home will be in New Holland, Ohio, but we're staying here until the college has the house and farm ready for us. Uncle Isaak and Aunt Helen and your cousins will be staying with us until we all move to New Holland where we will live in separate houses." Jake was happy to have his cousins in the same house, even though we would soon have to be moving again.

When both families were moved in and settled, the Warkentins upstairs and our family down, we had our first big meal together. In the blessing, Papa once again gave thanks to God and ended with, "Peace be to this house" (Luke 10:5). We needed that scripture, for though we now had much more room than we had in our shared house in China, we still had a house full of little boys (and big ones), as well as two toddlers, one ours, and one theirs.

Also, the whole first day, there was no peace, as we were to hear guns being shot outside, a terrifying sound to us children, who associated it with people we knew being shot in Russia.

"It's the first day of hunting season," explained Mama, "and people are out hunting pheasants, deer, rabbits, even wild turkeys. We want you to stay in the house so you won't be mistaken for a turkey, and shot by one of those hunters."

Then I was upset for the poor rabbits and other hunted creatures, but Papa said, "Remember, little Neta, it was only disguised as hunters that your uncles and I were able to escape out of Russia, and avoid being shot ourselves or put in prison."

All we had was $100. Papa and my uncles were given jobs cutting firewood for the winter. They were provided with crosscut saws, but Papa was good at improvising. He took the tires off the back end of our truck, and using a handmade wooden pulley wheel, belt, and sawblade, soon had a buzz saw that was much more efficient than the crosscut saw. Each time they had enough wood to fill a truck, they transformed the saw back into a truck, and delivered the wood.

On December 14th, Papa wrote a letter to his sister in Canada, saying,

> *Before I continue with my scribbling, we wish you the best of health and the peace of God. We are all well and healthy, including the children. Must inform you that we have received at our house, a small guest with the name Lydia. She is 18 days old. It seems not to matter whether in Russia, China, or America, they still come into the world in the same way. Hopefully, this one is the last, as we have six children. It is a big family and all healthy and chubby. Netgen was this time in the*

> *hospital. It was 11 days ... The birth at the hospital was better that the others were at home.*

Later that winter, May Schmidt was born to Aunt Anna and Uncle Abe, so that both families had six children. It began to look like a competition between our two families. Papa's letter went on:

> *Guess our relatives in Russia are having a pretty bad time of it. I don't know what will happen, it's as if the devil came from hell, and rules. Those Communists want it to be everywhere like it is in Russia. We have news from Harbin that many more (about 200 souls) have arrived, and our siblings (in Russia), are still afraid, or have not the price to travel. If I knew that our relatives were in China, even without a penny of money, then I would find some way to support them here, and they could come here, too. We could go into debt for them, as the money is worth a lot in China — $3.50 for $1.00, so if you had $50.00 in China, much could be done with it, not so?*

It was a harsh winter, but we were used to such weather. We were new at truck ownership, however, and learned the necessity of anti-freeze, which no one had warned us we would need.

Our 1928 Chevrolet truck that Papa converted into a camper for our trip across the United States. Makeshift toilet is to the left.

Children of the Aron and Isaak Warkentin families, and the Abram Schmidt family leaving Reedley, California, in 1931 to come to Bluffton, Ohio. The truck Aron converted is in the background. Back row, from left, George W., Helen W., Peter W., Abram S., and Agnes W. Middle row, from left, Peter S., John S., John W., Neil S., Isaac W., and Jacob W. Front row, from left, Alice W., and Alice S.

Chapter 14

Even The Animals Smiled!

"At last we're here!" I said to Helen, as we stepped into the white, two-story house near New Holland, in central Ohio, that we thought was going to be our permanent home. It was March 1, 1931, and just in time for our father and uncle to begin their job of managing the Bluffton College co-op farm. The new home of the Isaak Warkentins was a half mile down the road, and through a covered bridge that crossed North Fork Paint Creek.

"That creek is big enough to swim in!" I said, visualizing lying under shade trees on lazy, summer days and cooling in the rippling creek. We did occasionally get a chance to fish and swim but most of our time would be spent working on the farm and in the kitchen.

Bluffton College furnished the houses and barns, land, seed, and some equipment. The college got half of what we produced, and we got half. We grew wheat, oats, and corn, and raised horses, sheep, pigs, and chickens. We used the egg money to buy anything we couldn't grow in our garden. We also raised hay for animal feed.

Our house had a big kitchen with a wood-burning stove, where Mother made all our meals and Helen and I also cooked with her help. There was a pump on the kitchen counter with a dishpan underneath, and outside a windmill that pumped water to fill a trough for the animals.

"Life there was easy and happy," as Jake put it. "Even the animals smiled!"

We children once again had to attend a new school, and continued to learn English and teach it to our parents. There was a new sister to take care of, 2-year-old Alice, now running around getting into everything, and two mischievous boys, 5 and 7. Helen and I still had time to play in spite of the work. One of our favorite games with the neighbor kids was "Annie Over." We threw a ball or rag doll up over our shed, and it had to be caught by the kids on the opposite side. Annie was not supposed to hit the ground or land on the roof. If she landed on the roof, and came back to us, we yelled, "Pigtail!" and that was a point for the other side. If she hit the ground on the other side, it meant a point for us. We skipped rope, played hopscotch, and especially liked "ice box," a form of hide and seek.

I remember riding along when Papa delivered sweet corn and other produce to Critzers Canneries, in Circleville. We got to go through the factory and see how the corn was processed by machines, so differently than the way we helped Mother can at home. We didn' t go home empty handed, as Papa filled our truck with corn cobs for the animals. He never let anything go to waste.

Most of the time, though, when he went somewhere, he took Helen along instead of me, which made me angry. I felt he loved her more. One day, Papa said to me, "Agnes, Helen and I are going to the farmers' auction. Mother is busy with the baby and canning. You watch Jake, John, and Alice, that they don't get into trouble."

I was furious. I stomped my feet and announced loudly, "I'm going instead of Helen! John's a crybaby, let her babysit for once!"

Papa took me to the woodshed, as people did in those days, and instructed me, "Pick out a piece of wood, Agnes, and hand it to me." I did, and he used it to spank me.

Late that night when they came back from the auction, Papa woke me from a deep sleep, and said, "Agnes, I feel bad about you being angry with me, and about spanking you. You know I love you very much. The reason that I often take Helen with me, is that she can speak English better than you, and much better than I. She has a gift for it, and has learned so quickly. Today, when I nearly bought a boar with our hard earned money, she kicked me as a signal to put my money away. She had overheard the owner tell another man right in front of me that the boar was old and useless, and that he was getting a real bargain in the deal. The owner never dreamed that my child would be able to understand English, when I, her father, could not. She has a gift for languages. But you, too, have gifts. 'A merry heart doeth good like medicine,' " he quoted from the Bible (Proverbs 17:22), "and you, dear Neta, keep us merry, even in the darkest times. You have a gift for joy! And what about your sewing? That, too, is a gift from God, to be able to use your hands to make fine clothes for others, the way your mother does. 'Neglect not the gift that is in thee,' " he again quoted from the Bible (1 Timothy 4:14).

"Come, we'll get down on our knees and ask God to forgive us both, for things we have said and done this day" and we did. I learned later in life, that Helen didn't enjoy going to farmers' auctions, and would have preferred to stay home. She envied me.

In late fall of that year, when the harvesting was done, visitors from Bluffton College arrived, and told us we would have to move. Due to the Depression, Bluffton College had lost their farms and had to sell them. We would have to find jobs, and some place to live. We were all heartbroken.

Uncle Isaak and Aunt Helen did not like the winters in Ohio after living in Spokane, Washington's, mild climate, and decided to return to the west coast. They settled in Elk, Washington, where they farmed and drove trucks for a living.

Charlie French, a hardware store owner Papa knew, set Papa up with equipment and a wagon, as a section foreman on a 180-acre farm in South Solon, Ohio, not far from New Holland. Our farmhouse there was a yellow, two-story frame duplex that we shared with the Schmidt family, as they, too, had lost their job with Bluffton College. The house was up a long lane, and the log barn had been made 100 years before. Behind the barn, a railroad track cut the property in two.

That was the last house Papa lived in.

Chapter 15

I Fell Off The Gate

It was fun having a train run through our farm. We'd wave to the engineer and count the cars as they slowly rolled by and then wave to the men in the caboose. Sometimes, hobos would jump off and come to the back door to ask for food. It was the Depression, and many were out of jobs and hungry. Papa was a local welfare helper and always gave them something to eat. The old couch that we had used in our "camper" as we crossed the United States was now on our back porch. Papa would let them sleep there for a night and the next day they'd be gone on another train.

One day, our dog took a disliking to one of those hobos, and attacked him. Papa heard the noise and went and called the dog off before she had done much harm. He treated the wounds of the man and let him stay a while until he was sure the man was okay to go on.

After a few weeks, a railroad inspector came to the door and wanted to talk to Papa. It turned out that the man our dog had bitten had made a home in our cornfield among the shocks and then died there. Evidently, that hobo had been connected to a good family and the inspector was there to investigate the cause of the man's death.

We had an eighth of a mile walk down our lane to catch the school bus daily, and as we waited for our bus, a black car came by occasionally, and we children were asked questions about the man who had died. The inspector finally decided that neither our family nor our dog had caused the death of the man, and we no longer were bothered by questioners in black cars.

The trains not only brought us hobos; they increased our chances of field fires. One day, my parents, Helen, Jake, and I were raking the hay into piles in the fields as the train came slowly by, its coal-burning steam engine sending clouds of smoke up from its chimney. Sparks fell from the smoke into a pile of hay, and the dry hay burned quickly. I'd never seen my father so angry as he attempted to put out the fire. He never swore, but that day he shouted, "Hoof of the devil!" over and over. Later he apologized for his anger and his words, for he believed as the Bible says, we are to refrain from anger.

Besides growing hay for our horses, we also raised pigs on our farm. One day, Papa and Jake had noticed an old sow in the corner of the neighbor's field. She was nothing but skin and bones, and her long ears practically covered her face. She looked half dead as Jake remembered. Papa mentioned the sow to the neighbor and was told, "If you want it, take it," so Papa made a pen in the corner of the old log barn, and gave the sow a self-feeder trough and water trough. He pushed her head in, and she began to drink. He put a ring in her nose so she wouldn't root in the ground, and put rings in her ears and tied them back away from her face with twine so she could see. Within three months, she went from skin and bones to 300 pounds, and when Papa butchered her in the late fall, that was the most tender meat we had ever eaten.

That same year, Papa took Mama, Jake, and John to Springfield to the market where they sold twenty of our pigs, each 200 lbs. or more, for $20 each.

When they left, they drove through the town and parked across the street from the clothing store. They took John and Jake in and bought them the first store-bought clothes they had ever owned, double-breasted suits at $6 each that included vests and extra pairs of pants. Those were also their first Sunday suits.

On the way out of town, Papa stopped at a candy store, and bought hard candy, which we had never had, as Mother had always made cookies or cake for treats.

When they got home, Helen and I had dinner ready, and afterward, we ate the hard candy and sang the old German songs. It was almost like Christmas!

Besides pigs, we also raised curly horned sheep. Jake was fascinated with the large buck sheep. He had always wanted a pony to ride, and decided that that buck sheep was the next best thing. He tried to ride it several times, but Papa said, "Don't ride him anymore. If you do, I'll have to whip you."

Jake waited until Papa was working way back on the other side of the railroad track and wouldn't be back until suppertime. He made a halter out of binder twine, and jumped on the old buck sheep. The barn door was a "Dutch door," cut in half, the bottom was open and the top closed. The old ram took off with Jake on its back, and ran for the open door. However, the closed top portion was low enough to hit Jake in the head and knock him off the sheep's back. When he regained consciousness, he went crying to Mother.

"Jake, what happened?" she asked when she saw his head with its large bump rising. We all gathered around and sympathized.

"I fell off the gate," he told her, and she comforted him, and washed his head.

When Papa came home, he, too, noticed Jake's swollen forehead.

"I fell off the gate," he told him.

"Jake, you lied to me. Let's go to the barn." He had seen the twine harness still on the ram, when he put the horses in the barn. As Jake told us later,

> *Papa was strict! He whipped me because I did what he told me not to do, and I lied. When he punished*

you and hurt you, and you cried, he would cry with you (He was very sentimental), and that hurt more than the whipping! Then he took me to the house, and Mom found out I'd lied to her. She spanked me more than Papa, and I had no supper that night. The worst thing you could do to either of them was lie. Later, he took me down to the kitchen, and gave me food and apologized for hurting me.

On the farm, we also raised oats, corn, and wheat. Papa bought a Ferguson tractor for $50. It kicked like a mule, but could plow and harrow much more efficiently than our horses, which we still used for planting.

In threshing time, six or eight farmers worked together, using a threshing machine run by a steam engine that burned coal. All the farmers would go from one farm to another threshing wheat and oats. Threshing season lasted about two or three weeks. The women would gather and cook for all. Helen and I helped the women, and Jake carried water to the men in the fields.

When threshing time was over, Papa took us to the circus in South Solon. I was especially impressed with a ten-foot snake. The keeper threw a rabbit into its cage, and I watched while the snake swallowed it whole, somewhat the way I had imagined the "Black Dragon" might have swallowed us on our journey across its slippery back. I didn't know then, but soon we would be closely acquainted with death.

In December, Papa went on a trip with another man, to Bluffton, which was now about 120 miles away. When he got back, he had a terrible headache. Four days later, when he came in from feeding the pigs, he said his foot had fallen asleep, and then his whole right side did the same thing. It continued for about four days, and he fell a number of times, and shook on the right side. One day, he was coming to the house and couldn't find his way. Mother went and got him and put him to bed. Uncle Abe came and took him to Springfield Hospital, and then to University Hospital in Columbus, Ohio. They said they couldn't understand him.

"I will have to die," he told my mother at the time. "What a joy to die and live with God!" And yet at the time, he was only 35 years old, and none of us could understand why, after bringing us to safety in a new land, he would have to leave us now, completely on our own. It reminded us of the exodus of the Jewish nation. Moses led them out of Egypt, but was not, himself, to enjoy the benefits of the new land.

Papa died on December 17, and the doctors performed an autopsy, and discovered a tumor in his head. He was laid out in our parlor, and relatives and friends gathered, bringing food and sitting and visiting, and helping Mother.

At the funeral, some of the old German hymns were sung. Years later, going through some things Papa had sent her, his sister in Canada found and mailed us copies of music he had brought with him to America. He could not bring his fiddle, but fearing he'd have no music in his new country, he had brought his music. One of those hymns was sung that day:

> *Up, soul, up, leave the earthly pull.*
> *Grip your Savior's hand, in Him is the only joy.*
> *He banishes worries and pain. Leave the world and come*
> *Come, soul, come.* (Translated from German)

As Papa lay in the casket, and I saw his face for the last time, my thoughts were, "Why did he have to die? He worked so hard. I loved him so!"

A spray of white lilies were in his hands across his chest, and I cannot, to this day, bear the smell or sight of white lilies, even at Easter, as they bring back the horror of losing our Papa. At the graveside, as Reverend Kreider was praying the last prayers, large snowflakes began to fall, and it made me smile to think, "Papa would be pleased, as he loved the snow and cold climate of the land where he had grown up and spent most of his life. Snow was what he needed to accompany him on his final journey to be with God."

We sang Papa's favorite hymn:

Star on which I gaze
Staff with which I walk
Rock on which I stand
Leader that I trust
Bread on which I live
Spring where I can rest
My final destination
All, oh Lord, are you.
Without you I'd have no power,
Without you no ambition,
Who would lighten my burdens,
And keep us from falling apart?
Our faith, our hope, our love
All, oh Lord are you.
So I will continue in your way
With new songs joyfully come.
You are all, Lord, I need
Till the bells ring
And I am home. (Translated from German)

And Papa was truly home.

Aron Warkentin

Ebenezer Mennonite Church Cemetery

Chapter 16

Work!

On December 26, 1932, Mother wrote Papa's sister and family in Canada:

> *Forgive me for not writing to you right away. I don't know what to do, as Aron is dead. He died December 17.*

She explained what had happened and how, after Papa had died, the doctors had found the cause.

> *He was happy that he could die, but for us, we cannot understand why it had to be so early. We will go on — someone is giving us a chance to work — that way, we hope to keep going. The funeral was December 21, and we buried him at the Ebenezer Church Cemetery near Bluffton. We hope that the loving God will stay with us, as this puts me in a situation where I do not know what to do, or what I can do with my family. I am so alone. The neighbors have been, and are very helpful to us. The owners of the place where we live, gave each one of my family a Christmas present, but Christmas will never be the same. Pray for us that we can keep our courage up. I wish you the best of health, and that your greatest blessing and help will be with you until your family is on its own. Our children are all well. Please write. Have to close, will write more next time. A big greeting from your sister-in-law and children. Good-bye. See you again, if not here, then over there.*
>
> A. J. Warkentin

Mother was 32, knew very little English, and had no insurance or income. We had promised not to be a burden on the government.

"What are we going to do without Papa?" Jake asked after the funeral. Ever since he'd been old enough, Jake had followed Papa around the farm, learning from him about the machines and animals and all the work Papa was doing. Now he was lost without his role model, in a household of women and younger children. He began having nightmares and walking in his sleep. Some people wanted to separate and adopt us children, but Mother refused.

"No! I will keep them all together, and I will raise them all, myself!" she declared. To Jake's question, she said, "What will we do without Papa? Why, we will work!" In the end, it was work that saved us from being overwhelmed by grief. Life without Papa was unbearable, but with all the younger children around us needing care, we had time to grieve only through the hard work that led to exhaustion, and brought sleep and appetites in spite of sadness.

Mother began to develop an inner strength and calm she had not had before, a trusting in God's guidance and biblical promise, "I will never fail you nor forsake you." From then on, she often quoted Paul, "The Lord is my helper, I will not be afraid. What can man do to me?" (Hebrews 13:5-6 RSV).

Charlie French, the man who had set Papa up with farm equipment, took it back, and gave Mother a check for it plus a car. Mother had never driven a car and had to learn quickly. In those days, all cars had a stick shift, and I remember the discomfort of riding with her when the car jerked as she was learning to shift gears smoothly.

Uncle Abe and Aunt Anna Schmidt and our cousins moved back to the Bluffton area to farm; and the four Bluffton-area Mennonite churches moved our family into a house in their vicinity, and paid the rent until we could manage it ourselves.

We were able to live in that house until the owner's daughter got married and needed it for her home.

We then moved into a large white house on the Suters' property. It had plenty of room and a nice long porch but no electricity or indoor plumbing. The pump still stands outside the house as a reminder to younger generations that water had to be pumped in all kinds of weather and brought inside for household use.

Mother went straight to work refusing to rely on the charity of others. It was during the Depression and government flour, sugar, and other staples marked, NOT TO BE SOLD, were handed out by the WPA. Mother was adamant about not taking relief from anyone, not even the government. We raised broilers, and sold them in the town of Pandora, near Bluffton. By this time, we had a sow, three pigs, and a cow.

We four older children attended school together in a one-room school out in the country, and on Sundays the whole family walked to the Grace Mennonite Church in Pandora. When we were not in school, we all worked on Suters' farm, picking fruit and vegetables, hoeing, and harvesting. Anything left in the fields after the harvest, we were allowed to have, so we gleaned in the fields just as Ruth had done thousands of years ago in the fields of Boaz. We raked and scratched up anything left there, and also were allowed to have leftover fruit and vegetables that didn't sell at the Suters' farm market. In the evenings, after work, we canned beans, corn, and tomatoes. Carrots, beets, potatoes, and cabbages were stored for the winter in straw in an outdoor building. Besides the farm work and caring for our family, Mother also did housework in the Suters' home. Henry and Matilda Suter treated us all with respect. Jake remembered:

> *Mr. Suter was like a dad to me. He had the first rubber tire tractor in the area, a Ford; and I would*

ride with him on it, and he'd teach me about farming, until I got old enough to work on my own.

Later, Mother cleaned house for Mrs. Canfield, the wife of a banker in Pandora. "Mrs. Canfield spends a lot of time in bed," Mother said to us one day in a puzzled tone.

"What's wrong with her?" I asked. "Is she an invalid?"

"No, she just enjoys being there, I guess. I bring her coffee, and wash her coffee cups, and clean the dust balls from under the bed."

"Doesn't she know how to do those things herself?" asked Alice.

"Well, I suppose so. She just doesn't want to do them, and is willing to pay someone else; but why she can't think of other interesting things to do, I don't know."

"I'd read all the books in the library," said Helen, who had been listening.

"I'd have my own garden and animals to take care of," said John.

"I'd go rollerskating and have my own bike to ride," was my contribution. We all had what we thought were better things to do with our time and money than lie in bed and do nothing. For us, money was too hard to come by to waste on a maid for doing things we could do ourselves.

Often, when not working on Suters' farm, we kids gathered corn cobs that had fallen out of the corn cribs at the grain elevator. Then we'd go from farm to farm selling them for 10¢ a sack from an old, wicker baby buggy and a red wagon. We were so proud that we had enough to buy a loaf of bread or some other offering to bring home for the supper table that night. People used the corn cobs, in those days, as kindling for starting fires in wood-burning stoves and fireplaces.

Helen got a job cleaning at the Basingers' home for $5 a week, and gave all but a quarter to Mother for the family. I, too, had jobs, mainly on the Suters' farm and watching the other children in our family. One day, the boys and I had picked tomatoes on the Hiltys' farm, and were to deliver them to Hiltys' Market, five miles away. The tomato hampers were heavy, and I decided to make quick work of the five-mile trudge, by using Mother's car. I had never driven a car before but had watched Mother as she learned. She was at work and although I did not have her permission to experiment, it seemed like a good idea to use my initiative and save my little brothers and myself time and labor. The hampers had a point to them that fit very nicely into the groove in the fender, and when the boys stood on the running boards, one on each side of the car, they could hold onto the baskets of tomatoes with one hand, and onto a wire that ran between the headlights with the other hand. My inexperience in driving a car with a stick shift caused the boys and tomatoes to be bounced back and forth, bringing them close to being thrown off onto the road. Upon our bumpy arrival at Hiltys' Market, I received a lecture from Mr. Hilty who knew I didn't have permission to drive the car. He refused to let me drive home, and told my mother what we had done when she arrived after work to pick up the empty hampers. I was disappointed that neither Mr. Hilty nor my mother had appreciated my initiative and creativity in saving time and labor.

We did eventually get two horses and a wagon, and Uncle Abe made us a sleigh. Helen and I were permitted to drive the horses, so I felt a little better. I named one Buttons, and Helen named the other Maple, because, as she said, he was a sweet horse and the color of the maple syrup being made from the sap of the maple trees across the countryside around us.

In April of 1934, we were sad to receive a letter from Aunt Helen, in Elk, Washington, telling of the death of Uncle Isaak. He had been out on their farm plowing when he had

had a heart attack and died immediatedly. Like Mother, Aunt Helen was now faced with the responsibility of raising six children on her own as two more boys had been born into their family since they had left Russia.

Aron Warkentin and Abram Schmidt families, Pandora, Ohio, 1933. Front row, from left, John W., and Neil S. Second row, from left, Lydia and Alice W., and Mary S. Third row, from left, Jacob W., Mother, Aunt Anna S., Alice S., and John S. Back row, from left, Helen, me, Uncle Abe S., Abe S., and Peter S.

We lived in this house on Suters' farm near Pandora and worked for the Suter family after Papa died.

The first house we lived in when we came to Bluffton, Ohio.

Schoolhouse across from Ebenezer Mennonite Church, near Bluffton.

Ebenezer Mennonite Church, built in 1808.

Grace Mennonite Church of Pandora, Ohio, built in 1904.

Uncle Abe and Aunt Anna's house, where we got stranded one Christmas.

Chapter 17

The Chickens Will Have To Go!

There came a time when the Suters needed our rental place. We then moved into Mary Willard's house along Riley Creek. Her name always reminds me of chickens and chicken pox. Rent was collected, $10 a month, but the landlady was worried at having a family with six children in her rental house, so each time she collected the rent, she inspected it to see how much damage had been done. We had a long siege where each of us had our turn with chicken pox, so the house was in quarantine quite a while, and Mrs. Willard was frustrated that she could not come in for her usual inspection.

I don't know how Mother made it through that long siege, especially when we two older girls were sick and could not help with nursing the others. One invention of mother's was a game to get the younger children to cooperate during those long days in bed. She ran a string across the top of the room. Then she cut pictures of cars out of catalogs and wrote our names on them. She strung the cars up on the string and each day she moved forward an inch, the car of the child who behaved the best. At the end of the week, the child whose car was ahead, received a large orange. Oranges were scarce and expensive, and we were willing to try our best to get one.

Besides the long siege of chicken pox at Mary Willard's house, I remember the long winters, cold with lots of snow. At Christmas time, we put Papa's handmade harnesses on Maple and Buttons, and hitched them to the sleigh. The family bundled up in robes, and rode to Aunt Anna and Uncle Abe's to spend Christmas. The bells on the harnesses jingled just like in the song we had learned in school.

It snowed so much on Christmas Day one year, that the snow was piled high over their huge wrap-around porch, and we were snowed in for a number of days. There were oranges and candy and singing. Uncle Abe entertained the twelve of us children with his jokes and stories and games of hide and seek all over the house. If only Papa could have been there, it would have been a perfect Christmas. Finally, Uncle Abe was able to dig us out and drive us home on his mud sled as Mother had to get back to work at her job.

While Helen and I were getting a fire going in the pot-bellied stove, and the smaller children were hovering around to get warm, Mother went out to check the chickens. We hadn't expected to be gone so long, but a neighbor had promised to feed them if needed. When she got out to the chicken coop, Mother found there were only a few chickens there. There was no police department in our area in those days, but the mayor of Pandora, the closest town, handled all problems as well as he could. He promised to investigate and try to find our chickens. He knew everybody, and had an idea of who might be responsible. It did not take him long to find our chickens in the yard of a family a few miles away, a family known for their "sticky fingers." They were not punished, but we did get our chickens back and word got around about the family's theft. Sympathy was so great for our mother, a widow trying her best to raise six children, that the culprits eventually moved to another town.

A group of farmers in our area formed a co-op and built a tall ice house on Riley Creek, near us. In winters when the creek was frozen for weeks at a time, the ice became a foot or more thick. They scored the ice with a sharp tool and made a hole. Then, with a crosscut saw, they cut 1-foot-by-1 foot blocks and used ice tongs to lift the blocks out and load them on a sled. The sled was pushed through the snow in a chute to the ice house. There, a horse was hooked up to a rope and pulley, and when the horse walked, the blocks of ice were raised up and placed in a stack, and then covered with sawdust for insulation.

In the summer, farmers could go and get ice blocks as needed, if they had ice boxes, which were early refrigerators that required ice to keep food cold.

In the winter of 1935, it was very cold and stayed cold a long time. We did not go to Schmidts' that year for Christmas, they came to our house, as Uncle Abe had died of pneumonia the October before. We felt we had lost a second father, as he had been father to both our families since Papa had died. Aunt Anna was left to raise four boys and two girls, as a second girl, Mary, had been born to them in the United States.

The temperature that winter stayed cold until February, and we skated to school down the creek. There was an ice storm and our math teacher got all the kids out at recess to roll up balls of snow and place them in a row from the boiler room of our building and down the hill to a neighboring farm. We pumped water into buckets and a bucket brigade dumped the water between the snow balls to make a slick runway. Those who had sleds, brought them from home, and we all took turns sledding down our runway of ice.

We also played shin hockey in a pasture behind our barn, using a can for a puck, and a forked tree limb with a knot for a hockey stick. It was called shin hockey because cans were tin, and light-weight, hurting our shins when we got hit by one.

"If Uncle Abe were alive, he would have loved this winter. He would have been right out here playing with us," sighed John, who loved the snow and ice games, also.

Strange as it was, within five years of settling in the United States, the heads of all three of our families had died, Papa and Uncle Isaac, in their thirties, and Uncle Abe in his early forties. All three had left six children behind. Also, Papa's brother, Abel, died of pneumonia, and our Uncle John Warkentin died in Kansas. Their wives, who had always followed as their husbands led, were called on to lead and support their families as well.

Twice during those "growing up without Papa" years, we had had to get along without Mother, as well. Once, when she got pneumonia and was in the hospital, Helen and I had had to take over. We were afraid that authorities would adopt us out, but the people of our Mennonite church helped us and got us through.

The other time was when Uncle Abe died and Mother went to be with Aunt Anna and our cousins to help them out. As Jake remembered, "Helen was harder on us than Mom. She never talked much, but she knew how to use a stick!"

Mother had bought some turkey eggs at 25¢ each and a dozen had hatched. She told us not to feed them bread, as they wouldn't be able to digest it and would die. While she was gone, the younger kids sneaked slices of bread out of the kitchen, and had fun feeding them to the little turkeys, who loved their feast. Unfortunately, by the time Mother got home, all the turkeys had died. She never got turkey eggs again in spite of our protests.

We also had to give up our chickens. Our landlady had reason to be wary of us. During the coldest times in those long winters, Mother had brought the chickens into the house, and kept them on the third floor, moving those of us who usually slept up there, down to the second floor. Mrs. Willard eventually found out about this arrangement. "The chickens will have to go!" she announced. We were lucky she let us stay!

Chapter 18

All Spit And Polish, But No Heart

Eventually, we moved into the town of Pandora, Ohio, just a block from the school. It was a lovely graystone house on Jefferson Street, and had indoor plumbing. It also had a garden, but we were not allowed to have any animals there.

There was a Jot 'em Down Store in town owned by Mr. Allison. We kids took produce and firewood in for him to sell. One day, I saw a comb, brush, and mirror set I liked, and I took it home. When Mother saw it, she didn't say anything; but after supper, she said, "Come along, Agnes, bring the brush and mirror set. We are going for a walk." She was quiet and didn't punish me, saying simply, "I don't think it's right, do you?" She made me give the set back to Mr. Allison in person, and explain what I had done. I felt worse than if she had been angry or punished me.

There were many people in town who helped us. One day, some people brought a sack of food and placed it on our porch, but Helen saw them from the window and ran out.

"Don't you leave that here! We don't accept anything from anyone!" It turned out it was government food, and we were sensitive about accepting anything from the government, because when we had come into the United States, we had promised that we would be self-reliant.

Another day, the Reverend Mr. Whitmore came to call on Mother. "I hesitate to bring this up, Mrs. Warkentin, but at school, Miss Byers tells me your children are often hungry, long before lunch time. They've been caught several times sneaking bits of food from their lunch pails." (We children packed our lunch buckets each day before school, usually with bread, lard, fruit, and meat.)

"I can't believe they're hungry! I leave a big pot of oatmeal on the stove when I go off to work early in the morning," Mother told him.

After investigating, she discovered that by the time Jake and John were up and ready for breakfast, there was little oatmeal left in the pot. Hobos had been coming to the back door each morning asking for food; and being considerate of the needs of others, I had been too generous with our family's breakfast. Helen had been refusing to accept food from others, and I was giving food away.

Along with pride in self-reliance, our family took pride in keeping the house spotless. It didn't matter how old something was, you kept it clean.

In Pandora, I learned to ride a bike. My brothers had a bike, but we girls were not allowed to ride it. One day, I wanted to go uptown to the store, so I grabbed the bike, got on, and began to pedal. It seemed easy compared to my experience with the car. I got to the bottom of the sloping street, counting on the store's wall to stop the bike. I had not learned any other way to brake the bike. However, I had not counted on my body going on when the bike stopped, and I flew over the handlebars and through the store window, cutting my arms and legs with splinters of glass. I was once again in trouble with Mother.

Jake was not happy with me, either. "Neta, look at my bike now! It's a mess, and I expect you to clean it up and get rid of that dent. You did not have permission to ride it!"

"You remind me of a Russian soldier, Jacob!" which in my mind was the worst insult I could come up with, "All spit and polish, but no heart! You owe me a ride on the bike, which isn't just yours, you know. I've shared every toy I ever had with you."

John, who also owned the bike, laughed, marched up to Jake, and saluted. He, too, could get fed up with Jake's pompous and fussy temperament. Our screamer, at two, he had become a warm-hearted, easy-going person. I ironed Jake's shirts to his high level of perfection for a long time, as his way of getting even.

Jake got even with me still another time when I was in junior high, and clothes had become important to me. One day, I got the idea that I would wear one of Mother's long, flowing dresses to school and impress my friends. I picked my favorite, a flowered dress she wore to church. I got to school early, so I could sit with crossed legs in a leisurely fashion on the front steps at the entry to the building. As my friends and enemies arrived, there was oooing and ahhing at my adultlike appearance. My little brothers were there, however, among the spectators, and did not fail to give Mother a description of my early morning performance. I had to wash the dress, after suffering a severe scolding.

The summer I was fourteen, I got a job as a housemaid for a rich woman in Bluffton. She liked to sleep in each morning, and one of my jobs was to get her son up and feed and dress him. She had me dress him in knickers and a tam; and he had to be spotless all day. He had a pet lamb, and the two of them were a handful, even for someone who was used to kids and animals. Keeping him clean as he scampered around with his lamb was not easy. She had me iron and if she found a wrinkle in anything, I did it over until it was right. She used doilies on her furniture, and she taught me how to roll them up. I was glad when doilies went out of fashion.

After Lydia started to school and I was fifteen, Mother got a job on weekdays making negligees and underwear at Marvel Maid, a factory in Lima, Ohio. She carpooled with the neighbors, and she babysat for her room and board there; coming home on weekends.

She sewed for a living, but she continued to make our clothes as well. Two huge, rich ladies who had once taught school in Chicago, gave Mother two beautiful, royal blue coats and tams for us girls. Mother took the coats and remade them for Helen and me. Seeing us in church in our blue coats one Sunday, a church member commented to Mother, "My, your husband must have left you a great deal of insurance money to be able to buy such lovely coats for your girls!" We were more interested in what the boys thought of us in our royal blue outfits.

Helen and I were always eager to attend Sunday morning church, and even afternoon and evening services, as it gave us a chance to be with kids our age. Mother did not allow us to attend the public school dances or athletic events. There were quilting bees, where we women and girls got together a whole day at a time in order to handstitch a quilt. We worked at a quilting frame that folded up and was taken from house to house, as needed. We enjoyed sampling each other's recipes, and talking and laughing (Jake and John called it gossiping), but no boys were there. There were church picnics, ball games, and parties that the Mennonites attended as families, also. These, as well as church services, gave us the opportunity to socialize with boys. One night, after a church gathering, I stayed out later than Mother allowed. I was with a group of friends and I forgot to watch the time. I found her angrily waiting up for me when I got home. She kept a sharp eye on each one of us as tired as she must have been with her long hours of work.

Our little sisters were good at watching Helen and me, also. A boy named Harry Schroeder began walking me home from school and we would sit on the porch and talk, but little eyes and ears were always on us, as Alice and Lydia peered from the windows and heard everyting we said. I had a crush on Harry, or at least on his Model T Ford with the rumble seats. He began to pick me up at school. We took along my friends, too, and would drive around town; but Mother didn't disapprove, as he went to our church and she knew him.

Lydia and Alice

Me as a teenager

Front row, from left, Lydia, Mother, Helen, and Alice. Back row, from left, John, Jake, and me.

Pandora School where I modeled Mother's dress

Chapter 19

You Skated With My Date!

When I was seventeen and had graduated from high school, I began to work for a family with five children in Findlay, Ohio. I lived in their home and helped with the housework and the children. Also, I began to go out on dates with friends. One evening, I had a date with Claud Simmons. We went with my friend, Frances, and her date, Melvin Rice, to the Green Mill Skating Rink in Findlay. For some reason, Claud wouldn't skate that night, but Melvin skated with me a number of times and by the end of the evening, we had become friends.

"My sister and I work in the Findlay Cigar Factory," he told me, "but what I'd like to do is own a boat, and make a living on it," he confided. "The guys call me 'Boaty,' or sometimes 'Boots,' because of my high fishing boots. Where do you work?"

"I babysit for a family of five kids, and help with the housework, too."

"Do you like taking care of kids?"

"Well," I answered, "it's okay. I have four younger brothers and sisters. Can't say I'm not experienced with kids, but it would be nice to do something else, too. Guess I'd like to own my own store. Maybe sell sewing materials and do some sewing for people. I've been sewing since I was little, learned it from Mom, and it's what I like to do most."

"Agnes, it's getting late. Can I take you home?" he asked. I agreed, and he took me back to the Findlay house where I was staying. Melvin was living at his sister, Alta Sands' house, and when he got home, he went upstairs to his room. There was a knock on the door and Alta opened it to an angry Claud Simmons.

"Where's Boaty?" he demanded.

"He's upstairs, just a minute," she answered, leaving to call her brother.

"Boaty, come down here," yelled Claud, "bring my 82¢ with you!"

Melvin came halfway down the stairs, "What are you talking about? What 82¢?"

"You skated with my date all evening and you took her home. You pay the cost of her ticket, 82¢!"

"You weren't skating, remember? What kind of guy asks a girl to go skating, and then lets her skate by herself? Why did you ask her to go, if you weren't going to skate?"

"Eighty-two cents," Claud repeated, so Melvin tossed him the coins from his pocket, and called out as Claud left through the front door,

"It was worth it! Next time you take Frances!"

Melvin walked by the house a few weeks later, and asked me for another date to the Green Mill, this time without Claud and Frances. We kept right on skating together the rest of our lives!

Helen, too, had been dating, and within a year, she had married Dwain Hilty. Together they began farming: raising strawberries, tomatoes, sugar beets, and chickens.

In December of 1939, Melvin and I got a marriage license and on January 13, 1940, we were married by the Justice of the Peace in Findlay, Ohio. Melvin's sister, Estele, had a party for us afterward in her home.

During the party, there was no alcohol served, as they all knew my mother disapproved, so during the evening when someone handed me a Coke, I thought nothing of it. Evidently, someone had added something stronger to the bottle and it had its effect. Melvin and I were spending the night at his sister's house as we both had to work on Monday morning and had planned no honeymoon. Under the effects of the alcohol I had mistakenly consumed, I went upstairs and put on my nightgown, flannel though it was, being January; and I waltzed down the stairs with great abandon. Melvin and I danced, everyone cheered us on, and the party was a great success, in spite of the almost total absence of alcohol.

The next day, Melvin took me home to his family's farm near Pandora, Ohio, where we would live with his widowed father, Jim. His mother had died at the birth of her last child, and his brothers and sisters were grown and had homes of their own. I was used to living on a farm and doing farm work and Jim was always nice to me. I became cook for the two men, but was worried that my cooking would not be good enough to please them. One evening, Jim wanted ham and potatoes with jackets and gravy. In making the gravy, I got the flour too brown, and it was full of brown specks, but I couldn't throw it away. We never threw away food in my family. The stove was near the back door, and my father-in-law glanced into the skillet as he came in that evening.

"Girley," as he always called me, "you've made me sop gravy!" His genuine smile and delight surprised me. I had never heard of sop gravy. From then on, I was no longer nervous about cooking for him. In fact, Jim always was complimentary. He'd say, "Well, Girley, that'll do till something good comes along," and I knew he was pleased.

The kitchen in that home was good for something besides cooking. On cold winter nights, Jim got out his fiddle, and the young people would come across the fields to our home for square dancing on the bare wood floor. There was conversation and popcorn around the wood stove, and nobody thought it strange that the only drinks we served were fresh milk and water. How Papa would have loved to be there among us for the fiddling and conversation!

Also, on those evenings there were tales told of the Ottawa Indians who had lived in the area before the government had forced their migration west. Jim's place was on an old Indian trail that followed Riley Creek, but you had to leave the trail and hike up a lane to reach the house. When Melvin's sisters had been dating, he said their suitors would honk their car horns for them to come out, but Jim disapproved. "You want to date my daughters, you come to the house," he instructed them.

"Melvin's mother had died when his youngest sister, Violet, was only three. By then, his sister, Irma, was teaching in a one-room school. She asked permission to take Violet to school with her, and Violet went right on with the other kids and graduated before her sixteenth birthday.

I helped with the farm work and also continued babysitting and cleaning houses in the area, and Melvin started working for a construction company. We attended the Riley Creek Methodist Church where Melvin often sang in a quartet with his sisters.

We were happy there on the farm, but once in a while Melvin and I had our differences. One time in particular, I was really upset, but Melvin, as always, remained calm.

"When you've settled down, we'll talk," he'd said. I don't remember what the argument was about, but I took some belongings stuffed into my pillowcase and marched out. I walked to my mother's house in Pandora, planning to stay with her. As I approached her yard, she was out hanging up the wash. She saw me coming, and when I was close enough to hear, she called out to me, "Where are you going?"

"I'm coming here," I answered.

"No," she said, "where are you going?"

"Here," I repeated, annoyed.

"There's the pump. Get yourself a drink, and use the toilet," she pointed to the outhouse, "then get on home. If you have children and your husband dies, you can come here and live. Until then, your home's not here," and with that she dismissed me. I thought at the time that it was a harsh way to treat her daughter!

In 1942, when Jim got ill, and too old to work, he decided to sell the farm, since Melvin did not care for farming and preferred the construction work he was doing. Jim moved in with one of his daughters, and each of his children from then on took turns having him live in their homes.

Melvin and I moved into the town of Ottawa, Ohio, about ten miles from Pandora. A large brick house on Fourth Street had been made into apartments, and we rented one from Mr. Hauck for $9 a month. Our income was $16 a month. Melvin worked for Alberts Road Construction and Paving, which was a seasonal job; I worked at Frey's Department Store on Main Street. Upstairs, over the hardware supplies, they sold dry goods and sewing notions as well as other household items. Since I had sewn all my life, I knew all I needed to for the job. I made $5 a week.

When we moved to Ottawa, we were quite a distance, in those days, from the Mennonite church, so we began going to the Presbyterian church. It was a friendly church with a small congregation, but the members were active in the community and were like a large family that welcomed us and took us in wholeheartedly. Melvin joined the Kiwanis Club, and participated in their annual minstrel shows. I helped him dress up as a woman and he was a singing sensation!

At the same time that I was working for Mr. Frey, I worked for Dr. Eckelbarger, whose office was up the street from our apartment building. The woman who usually went with him on his rounds to deliver babies could no longer work for him, and he had heard me mention that in Russia and China my brothers and sisters had been born at home and that I was used to assisting with the procedure. He called and asked if I wanted the job and I was happy to get the extra work. He showed me how to tie the umbilical cord at both ends and cut it, and he showed me how to clean out the baby's mouth and eyes. I remembered watching my father deliver Alice in China, and never tired of seeing the tiny babies as they took their first look at the world from newly opened eyes. Often, I was the first person many of the children in town ever saw.

We had trouble with two deliveries. One was a baby born with the cord around her neck, and the doctor's tone of voice was enough to let me know the child's life was in danger as he instructed me to flip her over quickly to disentangle her. The other difficult delivery was a child in the uterus sideways, and I watched, amazed, as Dr. Eckelbarger turned that baby around while it was still inside the mother's womb.

Me in the new outfit I bought with money from my job.

Melvin's family church, Riley Creek Methodist Church, where he sang duets with his sister.

House in Pandora where we lived when I was going with Melvin.

Bridenbaugh Schoolhouse where Melvin went to school, now a museum where there is material on the Rice family.

Chapter 20

I Feel Like A Secret Agent!

We began to hope for babies of our own, but I had a series of miscarriages in the next few years. At the third miscarriage, I was very sick and needed a hysterectomy. My employer at the store, Mr. Frey and his wife, Orchid, had always been supportive of me, giving me confidence in myself and my ability to work; so when I was desperate for the $500 needed for my operation, I went to Mr. Frey and asked if he would lend me that amount. He readily agreed, and I was able to pay it all back, a little at a time. I built up credit in the town without ever planning to.

Melvin worked at the sugar mill in Ottawa, where they processed sugar beets grown in the area, but that, too, was a seasonal job like the construction work. Eventually, he was able to get a job at Sylvania, a plant that employed him until he was ready to retire. It was a steady, year-round job for 78 cents an hour. We were so tickled with such a great salary and with the fact that the job was year-round.

We rented our first house, on Second Street, a gray, wood frame, comfortable home beside the railroad track. It was there that I had a terrible fright. Melvin was a hunter. One day, he went into the bedroom to get his gun to clean it. I heard a shot, and then, silence. I ran into the room expecting to see Melvin's body on the floor, but instead, he stood there gazing opened-mouthed, at a huge hole in the ceiling.

"It was supposed to be unloaded," he muttered sheepishly. I turned and left the room silently knowing that anything I said might get me in trouble.

Working at Frey's Store, I got to know the people in town fairly well. One was a prominent gentleman who came in daily. One day, Mr. Frey asked me to watch him carefully.

"Don't take your eyes off him while he's in the store, and if you see him take anything, give me a nod."

I did as Mr. Frey had asked, and saw the man take several tools and put them in his pocket. I gave Mr. Frey a nod, and as soon as the gentleman had gone out the door, Mr. Frey was out there with the customer asking him to empty his pockets and return what he had taken. This happened daily, and I marveled at my employer's patience and compassion at not turning him in to the police.

Another customer had a similar habit, and one day, one of the sale bikes Mr. Frey had parked out on the front sidewalk of the store, was missing. When an employee told us who had been into the store that morning, we all thought, "Surely she wouldn't have removed something that large in broad daylight!"

"Agnes," Mr. Frey suggested, "how about you and Mary walk home past that woman's house, and see if you can catch sight of that bike."

So we did, and sure enough, there it was, parked in her garage with the door wide open. Most of us worked so hard for the money we got; it was difficult to believe a person who had all she or he needed would take things from the store without paying for them.

On one of our walks home, Mary and I were summoned by Mr. Finster to the door of his meat market. "This meat didn't sell, and it won't keep. Can you find a use for it?"

We certainly could, and we gratefully did. From then on, he often stopped us when he had meat he couldn't keep, and it was a welcome addition to our supper tables, especially since it was during World War II and many things were becoming scarce.

Our brother, Jake, had joined the army, and had a desk job in the United States. We were relieved that he hadn't been sent overseas.

Our younger sisters, Alice and Lydia were in high school, and had jobs at the A&P Grocery Store after school and on weekends, but did not always work the same hours. Neither did they always get along or agree about everything. One time, Alice had laid out her clean clothes before work, so she'd be ready to change and go out on a date when she got home from work. Lydia got home first, put on Alice's clothes, and went out herself. When Lydia got home later, she had an angry sister to deal with. Most of the time, however, they were inseparable.

Our prayers for a child had ended with my hysterectomy, but God was not yet through with my petitions. From a friend we learned of an adoption agency where there were files of children desperately needing homes. Through the agency, we were able to arrange the adoption of a newborn baby boy. He was only five days old when we arrived at the Van Wert Hospital, pieces of gunny sack covering our license plates, as recommended to us, for confidentiality.

"I feel like a secret agent involved in espionage," Melvin confessed. It was the happiest day of our lives. We were thrilled to have a child of our own, after all the agony of miscarriages, and hoping, and then loss of hope. We named our little blond, blue-eyed son, Dale Edward Rice.

Me, Melvin, and Dale Edward Rice

The first home Melvin and I rented in Ottawa, Ohio

Chaper 21

A Race Track Is No Place To Raise Kids!

That same year, in 1944, we saw our brother, John, once our crybaby, off to war. In August, he had joined the Coast Guard Merchant Marines, and because of the war, it was under the authority of the Navy. He was only 17. This time, we were the ones who cried. It was hard to see our mischievous, fun-loving little brother go off on a life-threatening mission. The thought that we might never see him again was always with us.

He was first sent to New Jersey for training and then overseas to Europe. It was strange that for his first trip out of the United States since we had immigrated, his destination should be back to Russia, the place we had escaped from just fifteen years before. As an American citizen, he was returning on a mission to help the Russians in their struggle against Nazi Germany.

We were all, by then, Americans. We children, being under 18 at the time, had automatically become citizens, when Mother had taken the oath of allegiance on November 18, 1937. Helen had done a good job of teaching her to read English, and Papa, I'm sure, was proud of us all. I think he was smiling on John as he went off to war for his country, also. We were a family big on paying back our debts and it was one way of saying, "Thanks!" to a country that had taken us in and given us freedom.

John was assigned to a ship delivering supplies to Allied troops. He described later, his first assignment:

In December, 1944, we left port from Redhead, New Jersey, on Christmas Eve. Upon leaving, we were issued cold weather gear: fur-lined boots, insulated underwear, etc., with the understanding we were bound for Mermansk, Russia, a coal mining district in the Arctic Circle, to deliver supplies to the Russian government. Due to severe cold weather (20 degrees below 0), and 30-foot waves, and the very real threat of German U-boats, we already had lost large equipment that was shackled on the deck. We had escorts, but no radar. At the last minute, the command rerouted us to Belgium, since Antwerp and Brussels' seaports had been secured by the Allied troops. We went on to Holland by canal, where a bomb hit the locks, and then on to Brussels, where we unloaded our cargo, with the understanding that it would be shipped overland to the Russian troops. Our cargo consisted of clothing, food, tanks, bombs, and trucks.

In the two-and-a-half years that John was in World War II, his ship made seven supply deliveries across the ocean, all the time under the threat of attack of German bombs from Messerschmitts and torpedoes from German submarines.

"When we landed on Omaha Beach after the invasion, the area from the beach to Sherbourg Forest looked like an enormous graveyard, " he told us later.

After the war in Europe ended, John's ship was assigned to haul surplus supplies from Europe to forces still fighting in Japan. Traveling through the Mediterranean Sea, their ship stopped in Italy and Egypt, giving the crew a chance to go ashore. Our brother, who had traveled the world as a 2-year-old, climbed to the top of the Tower of Pisa, and rode a camel to the pyramids near Cairo. For once, he would have memories of his travels to tell his children one day.

Their brief respite from war was interrupted when their ship passing through the Red Sea on its way to the Far East, hit a mine that damaged the front of the ship and injured a number of the crew. John spent thirty days in a hospital in Calcutta, following an operation, due to his injuries. Foreign hospitals welcomed American patients as the United States paid them more than other countries.

When the war ended, thousands of military people were headed home at the same time. Beginning April 1, John was stranded at the bus station in Washington, D.C., for three days, waiting in line for room on a bus. Behind him in line, someone kept bumping him with a large box. Finally, he turned around and pointed out to the woman that she was jabbing him in the back with her box. "Well, how about holding it for me, so it won't keep jabbing you in the back?" she said.

As they began to talk, they found that they were both going to Ohio, and both had worked for the U.S. Coast Guard. Myrna Taylor worked as a clerk in Washington tracking the supply shipments, and John, working on one of the ships she tracked. After three days of waiting and talking in the bus station, John and Myrna traveled back to Ohio together.

By April 4, 1946, John was home from the service. It had been a long and very tense two-and-a-half-years for all of us. To have him back well and strong was an answer to our prayers. Twice we had had to have patience, and twice we had been blessed, once with a healthy, growing son, Dale, and now with the safe return of John. Why was I so slow to trust in God's answers to my prayers?

John introduced us to Myrna, beautiful, and, like John, fun to be with. They made a handsome couple, John with his short, blond, Navy haircut, and mischievous smile; Myrna, with long, dark, curly hair, and ready laughter. Mother disapproved, saying she was too worldly, and not his type; but I liked her from the start. I discovered she loved dogs and horses, and would rather be cleaning out the barns and pitching hay than working indoors. So much for sophistication!

On April 13, John borrowed our 1940 Chevy truck, we thought, to take Myrna back to her home in Columbus, Ohio. When he returned home, he went to Swanton, Ohio, to help Dwain and Helen do the spring planting. One night, we had a family gathering, and Helen noticed somthing wrong with John. Taking him aside, she said, "Johnny, you're not yourself, tonight. Where is our fun loving brother?"

"It's not much fun without my wife. You know that truck we borrowed from Agnes and Melvin? Well, we didn't go to Columbus, we drove to Covington, Kentucky, had blood tests, got a license, and a preacher, and got married."

"Well, I guess if you're old enough to risk your life for our country, you're old enough to get married. Congratulations!" Helen said, "But what are you doing here? Go get her and bring her back." John had just passed his 19th birthday.

We didn't know it until later, but John and Myrna had decided on the bus to marry, even though they'd known each other only a few days. They had known each other only 13 days when they had gotten married.

When John got back with Myrna, they asked Dwain and Helen if they could have the unused chicken coop to fix up for a home and Helen and Dwain agreed. We were all amazed at what they were able to do with that chicken coop to make it into a comfortable home. They lived there two years; then moved to Columbus, Ohio, where they bought and bred thoroughbreds and quarterhorses. Myrna raised and trained them, and she and John traveled to fairs and race tracks to race them.

In 1951, when Myrna became pregnant, they decided to give up traveling. "A race track is no place to raise kids!" said John and Myrna agreed. Helen and Dwain gave them an acre of their 120-acre farm near Swanton, where they moved their horses and hired a trainer. John began a career as a plumber. After their third child was born and their horse trainer suddenly died, they no longer raised race horses, although they always kept horses for riding in the area. Eventually, they bought a large farm adjacent to Helen and Dwain's, where John farmed and raised livestock, as well as ran his plumbing business, doing work for large construction companies. Myrna became a township trustee, and later a member of the county health board. They had been married 57 years when Myrna died.

They met on April Fool's Day, married April 13th, had only known each other 13 days when they married, and started out married life in a chicken coop. So much for superstition!

THE UNITED STATES OF AMERICA

TO BE GIVEN TO
THE PERSON NATURALIZED

No. 4368990

ORIGINAL

SECURELY AND PERMANENTLY
AFFIX PHOTOGRAPH HERE

Seal

DEPARTMENT OF LABOR

Mother's Certificate of Citizenship, November 18, 1937

Myrna and John Warkentin in front of their first home, which they converted from a chicken house on Helen and Dwain's farm.

Mother, Dale Rice, and me holding Patty Leonard, at the Ottawa Presbyterian Church.

Melvin singing in a local minstrel show. Best legs in town!

Chapter 22

Can I Have Your Name?

By the time Dale was old enough to start to school, we had bought a home on West Main Street, within walking distance of the elementary school and the Ottawa Presbyterian Church. It was one of the earliest houses built in Ottawa, a fine, old brick house near the Blanchard River that ran through our town. It was a double and my mother moved into the other side. She had started working at The Cozy Corner Restaurant on Main Street in Ottawa; so it was an excellent location for her, and we enjoyed having her near us and helping with our son.

Melvin and I remodeled the house, painting, papering walls, and putting in a beautiful open stairway and new carpet.

"Melvin," I said one day, "I've come a long way from that straw hut in China! We've done a good job on this house, and I love it, especially the bathroom! Such luxury!" Evidently, Dale thought so, too. On his first day of school, by midmorning, he was back home on our doorstep.

"Dale, why aren't you in school? You can't just walk out when you feel like it! You need to stay all day with the other kids."

"I know," he replied, "I just came home to use the bathroom."

"There are bathrooms at school, Dale," I explained.

"I know, the teacher showed us, but I don't like them. Ours is special." It took a couple of trips back to school with Dale in hand to convince him he wasn't going to get by with his trips home to use our "special" facilities.

All of Melvin's brothers and sisters had taken turns having Jim Rice live with them at their homes. Now it was our turn, and we enjoyed having him. It was particularly nice having him so that Dale could get to know him well, and they became good friends.

One day, Mrs. Hampton from the adoption agency called us, "Would you be interested in adopting another boy?" she asked. "He's five years old, and we are having difficulty finding a family who wants a child that age. He's been in one foster home after another, waiting his turn to be adopted. I must warn you, he's not in the best of health at the moment."

"We're leaving on a fishing trip soon, but I'll talk it over with my husband and let you know," I told her. Melvin and I discussed it, and our only reservation was that two active boys might be too much for Jim, who was now in his eighties. Jim assured us he'd raised a big family and was used to a lot more than two children. We decided to take the boy along on our trip, get acquainted, and see how we all got along. Then we'd make a decision.

Mrs. Hampton brought the child to our home on the day we were to leave for the lake, and we were in for a shock. He looked like a war orphan poster child, malnourished and obviously neglected, with a smile that revealed his need for dental work.

We had started out on our journey toward Houghton Lake in Michigan, pulling Melvin's fishing boat behind us, when our little guest spoke up. "You going to keep me?" he asked.

"I don't know," was Melvin's honest answer.

"Can I have your name?" was the child's next question.

"Are you sure you want to be called Melvin?" my husband asked.

"Well," he thought a minute, "what's your middle name?"

"Ray. My name's Melvin Ray Rice. What name would you like?"

"How about Thomas Ray Rice? I like that," he decided. "That way, I'll have your name, and a name of my own." That little fellow put down roots fast!

When we got to our campsite at Houghton Lake, we were busy setting up for the night, and the boys wanted to fish, immediately. When Melvin didn't fix Tommy a fishing pole right away, he went out, got himself a long stick, and a safety pin, and made his own fishing pole. He was used to fending for himself.

After our trip, Mrs. Hampton came to discuss the possibility of Tommy's placement with us. Jim had warned us after seeing Tommy that because of his very poor health, we shouldn't become attached to him, as he probably would die. There was no question about our decision, however. We were already attached to him; we had fallen in love with him and wouldn't have given him back for the world. We needn't have worried about Jim's coping with the boys. They all got along fine. In fact, Jim stayed with us the longest of any of his children, remaining in our home until he died at the age of 93.

My mother enjoyed Tommy's company, too. The Weatherseal Plant had opened in Ottawa in 1948, and Mother got a job there. She ran the kitchen and prepared meals for the plant's employees. She also joined our church and enjoyed being able to walk there.

One day, she had to make a trip to pick up baked goods in the nearby town of Leipsic. She wanted to take Tommy along for the ride, as she had in the past, but this time she went one way and came back another. Tommy noticed, and thinking they were not returning to Ottawa, he figured she was taking him away from us. He would not go on errands with her again for a long time.

When Tommy came to us, he was ready for the second grade. We took him to the doctor, and discovered he was not only malnourished, but had rickets as a result. His teeth were in terrible shape, also. We hoped he was getting treatment in time to still become a healthy child. Fall came, and he started to school. We weren't worried, as he had adjusted well to us and the town over the summer. Also, we knew what a bright little boy he was and how much he could do on his own. When he brought home his first grade card, however, he had received all *D*s and *F*s. I took the grade card to school, and had a conference with his teacher, Miss Malcolm.

"First of all," she explained, "he can't write with his right hand. Also, he's color-blind and cannot read. I had this second grade group in first grade, and they are all together in the same place in reading. I've whipped them into shape, just the way I want them, and Thomas does not fit in."

I tried to explain that Tommy had been in a number of foster homes and different schools and might need time to come up to her expectations, but we would work with him at home.

"Isn't it a shame that nice people like you adopt children like this?" she asked, but at that remark, I was too angry to answer. I realized she was against adoption, period, not Tommy, in particular.

I was so angry, I walked out, but not away from Tommy's problem. I went to the principal, but he backed up the teacher and did nothing. I then talked to Mrs. Hamptom at the adoption agency and learned that in Tommy's class there were three other newly adopted children who were not "fitting in" to Miss Malcolm's class either; a little boy in the McGinnis family and a set of twins in the Fischer family. I went to the school board meeting and presented my problem, mentioning the other families, whose newly adopted children were also suffering from their teacher's lack of compassion.

A week later, Melvin came home with the news, "I just had an encounter with Miss Malcolm at Finsters' Market. She said to me, 'You've got a wife with a temper!' I answered her back, 'You going to start in on me, now?' "

At times, my temper has come in handy. Tommy got no more *D*s or *F*s.

Aganetha Wiebe Warkentin (mother) when she moved to Ottawa, Ohio.

Dale, me, and Tommy Rice in 1957

Tommy Ray Rice

Chapter 23

Another Black Dragon!

Where we lived in northwest Ohio, a glacier had once advanced down from the north, leaving the land flatter and richer than the rest of the state. When it melted, our area had become part of the Great Black Swamp, and would still be swamp today, if the farmers had not inserted drainage tile under the ground to remove excess water.

In the spring of 1950, it rained in record amounts, adding to the rivers and creeks already swollen by melted snow, and the Blanchard River, our near neighbor, overflowed its banks. Day by day we watched it creep toward our house, and we began to move any furniture we could up the stairs. People traveled around town in row boats. Manhole covers popped like Tiddley Winks leaving deep holes in the street hidden under the flowing water. Signs around town shortened, as their poles disappeared under the flood waters, and a log floated by our kitchen window bearing a snake that had found refuge there.

"Another Black Dragon!" I cried to Melvin, "only this one is not sleeping like the last. Oh, Melvin, our lovely 'new' home will be ruined in a day or two!" And it was. The river came right up to our windows and moved in, covering our new carpet and stairway, and our newly papered walls.

Alice and her husband, Junior Frey, came in a boat to remove mother and us from our upstairs rooms, and we wept. The Blanchard River was our "Black Dragon."

It only stayed a few days, but when it receded, it left dead animals and rotten plants in people's yards. It left a muddy scum and a bad smell. The street was lined with ruined furniture and books and home-canned goods, no longer safe to eat. All was thrown into trucks by silent people and taken off to a local dump.

Inside, it was even worse. We cleaned off the scum, but the smell would not go away. We hadn't the money to buy new carpeting and replace the warped woodwork. We just wanted to leave and not go back. But who would want to buy our house in its condition? And where would we go if we could sell it? We addressed these questions to God, who had guided me all my life, and both questions were answered for us. The first came with a single man wanting to move out of his sisters' home. He and his two single sisters had had a falling out, and he was in a hurry to find a place to live. He came to our house with cash in hand and offered us more than we had hoped to get for it, but he said we would have to be out within two weeks.

We not only had to find another place to live but within two weeks. With two boys, and so many places damaged by flood waters, how could we move in two weeks? The answer came in the form of another man in town, Scoot Morman, who remodeled old houses, and had an apartment available in part of a large house on Maple Street. We could rent it while we built a house of our own, this time away from the river. We rented the house on Maple Street, and used some of the money from selling our house to buy land to build a new house.

My mother stayed with relatives for a while, but she was used to being independent and did not want to live with anyone. She found another place to rent and eventually built a house near the Weatherseal Plant.

Aunt Anna would have been proud of Mother had she been there to see the change in her since Papa had died. When raising six children, our mother had had to take a firm position and refuse to be moved from it.

One of Mother's first visitors in her new home was her sister, Maria, who had been living in Paraguay, and had gone to visit relatives in Canada, and then stopped in Ohio to see us. My brother, Jake, had come to visit and was full of questions for her.

"Aunt Maria, I know the story of how we escaped from Russia. How did you get out? Was your trip dangerous?"

"No," she said, "I'll tell you why. A long time ago, the Russians under Stalin took my husband to a forced labor camp, and he was never released, just like our mother, your Grandmother Wiebe, who was taken to the salt mines and forced to work until she died there. My sons and I were treated so badly by the Communists, that when the German troops came into our town, we thought of them as friends. My two sons joined the German Army, and I became the mistress of a German SS officer. He gave me plenty of money so that eventually, I was able to leave, and immigrate to Paraguay, where my sister and her family live."

As Maria told her story, the shadow of marching soldiers passed across my mother's face, and her body stiffened. "Nazis! Just as bad as Reds!" she muttered, and then, "Pack up!" she snapped, "you're leaving. You're not staying another night under this roof!" As soon as Maria could get her things together, Mother loaded her and her bags into the little blue coupe, drove her to the bus station, and put her on a bus out of town. We never heard from her again.

The first house Melvin and I bought and renovated, but we were flooded out.

We rented part of this house after the flood in Ottawa.

The house we built after the flood.

Chapter 24

I'll Mind My Own Business!

I learned from my mother's example that women can take the initiative and support their families in a time when most American women stayed home and took care of house and children. Melvin was in a car accident and unable to work. There were lots of doctor bills piling up and there was no question of going on welfare. My mother and sister, Helen, had set too good an example for me. "No, you don't do that!" echoed in my mind from past years. I was working at Gambol's Store for Clark James, and knew there must be some way to make more money. Dale had graduated from high school and married, but there was still Tom at home, and Melvin and me to support. Melvin went back to work but couldn't do the work anymore. One day he had climbed a water tower to do some maintenance work, but had had to back back down, leaving the job unfinished. He was treated for hardening of the arteries but did not improve.

I heard my father from the past, "Neta, you are gifted in sewing, just as Helen is gifted in language. Use that gift now!"

So, just as he had learned new jobs in China when he couldn't farm, so I could learn a new job, too. I had heard of a woman in Findlay, Ohio, who taught professional sewing, so I went to her every day for four weeks and learned to make custom-fitted draperies and bedspreads, dust ruffles, and pillow shams. I learned to measure and make fan-folded pleats. I climbed ladders to the ceiling and installed rods and hung drapes. My teacher was Nellie Baker, and oh, she was good! I'd go home from one of Nellie's lessons and say to myself, "There ought to be a short cut," and I'd try it my way, but inevitably, I'd end up having to rip it out and do it Nellie's way.

After I completed my training, Tom asked me one day, "What're you going to do now?"

"I'll mind my own business!" was my answer. I opened my business in our home, so I could be with Melvin and also work. I hired two women to work with me, Kay Slant and Katherine Busher. I would go to customers' homes and install the rods and drapes. Tom helped with this when he wasn't in school.

One day after we had installed new, fan-folded pleated drapes for a prominent customer, she declared she didn't like the way they looked. We took them home but for the life of me, I couldn't see what could be improved in them, nor could Melvin or Tom. Carefully, I folded them, and laid them aside. After a week, the lady callled and said, "Am I ever going to get my drapes?"

"They're done," I replied, "I'll bring them right over."

I packed them into the car, drove to her house, and installed the drapes, just as I had before, and she exclaimed, "That's just what I wanted!"

I smiled and said, "Thank you for your business!"

One afternoon, while I was working on some drapes, two of my friends, Adrianna and Laura Miller, stopped in. They were both smoking.

"What does your mother say about that?" I asked, knowing what my mother would say if I smoked.

"She doesn't know," answered Laura.

"We just don't tell her," added Adrianna.

"Well," I laughed, "I'm sure we all do things we don't tell our mothers. Come on in. I'll get some coffee."

They followed me to the kitchen, and we sat around the table with our coffee and some blackberry pie I had made the night before.

"Do you remember that woman I was telling you about who asked me to redo her bedroom with bedspread, pillow shams, and matching drapes? She picked out beautiful, expensive material — the best; and after she'd had them for a month, she brought them back, and said she decided they weren't what she wanted after all."

"I remember and they were drapes cut to fit her windows. Who's going to want those?" Adrianna asked.

"Had she paid you yet?" asked Laura.

"Just the down payment," I said. "They get a month to pay the rest; her month was up!"

"Isn't she the one who insisted you send the bedspread to a factory in Toledo, where she used to live, to have it specially quilted?" asked Adrianna.

"Yes," I answered.

"Who is this woman?" Laura asked.

"Never mind, you don't need to know, but aren't some people strange? I was in the Columbus Grove furniture store yesterday and telling my annoyance to Mr. Higgins, the owner, but I didn't mention names.

" 'Oh, I know her,' " he said, " 'she's done that here. She bought all new living room furniture from our 1/2 Off Sale, entertained some important people in town, and then had it returned to the store, saying her husband said it didn't fit in right. Even had our men move her old stuff back downstairs while they were there.' "

"At least he could resell his furniture. Maybe you can find someone who'll buy the bedspread and has similar or smaller windows," suggested Laura.

"But you should be paid for having to alter the drapes, if they can be altered to fit. What she's doing isn't right!" said Adrianna.

"I think I'll talk to her husband. He's busy with his work and may not even be aware of what she's doing," I decided. He did eventually pay me a fair amount of the cost.

When Adrianna and Laura had gone, I noticed half a pack of Pall Mall cigarettes left on the kitchen table, and I decided to try my first cigarette. I was surprised that it didn't bother me since I had heard that it made some people sick their first time. I went back to my sewing room, taking my cigarette along, and balanced it on the side of a saucer while I worked.

As I was hemming the drapes by hand, something in the mirror in front of me caught my eye. Smoke was rising from the lovely damask drapery material spread in ripples of blue and green on my work table. As the cigarette had burned, and shortened, it had become unbalanced and tipped over onto the cloth, making a hole, ringed with black edges. I had ruined only one piece of drapery but had to replace all the material, since I couldn't get the same dye lot as before. It cost me $48, a lot more money than it is today; but it turned out to be a good investment, as it was the last cigarette I ever smoked.

Chapter 25

Just Like Mrs. Canfield!

It was a good business and a good source of income for twenty years. During those years, Tom graduated from high school and married his high school sweetheart. His engineering courses at the University of Toledo were interrupted by his two years in Vietnam in the medical corps rescuing wounded soldiers by helicopter. He received the Purple Heart for injuries suffered in the TET offensive. Like his Uncle John, his grandfather, and great-grandfather, he had served in the medical corps, saving lives instead of taking them. He returned home to his wife and a son he had never seen and then finished his engineering courses to become a radiologist.

Eventually, Melvin's health got worse. He began to have problems with his mind, forgetting things, and complaining about how dumb he was for forgetting them.

"I'm nuts! What do you want?" he'd say in frustration. One day I came home, and when I opened the garage door, I found him on the floor beside two black tar cans with a belt around his neck. He had tried to hang himself but had fallen in the attempt. I sought counseling from our pastor asking him to talk to Melvin, but I was not able to accept the advice he had to offer. "Put Melvin in a nursing home," he advised, "and divorce him. Then you can get on with your life."

I could not follow his advice. I found that God had a creative idea for me that fitted our situation. I gave up my business, sold the house, and we moved to a cottage at Russells Point on Indian Lake where Melvin could keep his boat, and spend his time fishing, a life he'd always dreamed of living. I wasn't sure how I'd support the two of us, but once settled in, we were approached by a man offering us a job delivering the newspaper on a rural route, the car being provided. We would also be paid extra to insert a shopper section for merchants in the area. It was the job we needed, as I would have Melvin with me, and he would be able to help by placing the papers in the roadside tubes as I drove. The job got us both out of the house, and made Melvin feel useful again.

We delivered the papers for eight years until Melvin was no longer able to help. At that time, he was diagnosed as having Alzheimer's disease. We knew then that he would get progressively worse.

We moved back to Ottawa, Ohio, into a new apartment in a retirement community, called Tawa Manor, where I was able to earn a salary as assistant to the manager of the apartments, helping the residents there. I would be close to Melvin and be able to take care of him, also. His disease had been a blow, but God was always with us, guiding us, and providing for our needs. Eventually, Melvin became more than I could handle and had to be placed in a local nursing home.

I retired from my job as assistant manager in 1988 but continue to work, sewing and doing alterations in my home. Doing what I like to do most and visiting with those who bring me business make my life full and interesting.

Mother worked at the Weatherseal Plant for twenty years but also made pies for a local restaurant in the evenings when she got home. There came a time when she had an illness, and the doctor recommended she go to the Putnam County nursing home temporarily for full-time nursing care.

When she had recovered, my sister, Alice, arrived at the nursing home and announced, "I've come to take you home to live with us, Mother."

Our mother replied, "What for? I'm not moving. I have a private room, which I've never had before in my life. They dust under my bed, bring me coffee and meals, wash my dishes

THANKS FOR A GREAT TIME DEB.

THANK YOU MIGUEL + ALEX + MAYA FOR SHARING YOUR MOM.

LOVE YOU ALL

GRANDPA Jack

A note from

Pat Kaple

— I'm just like Mrs. Canfield here!" and she enjoyed being waited on there, until death several years later. She lived her last years, as she saw it, in style and comfort, seeing her children well and on their own. She lived to see Dale and Tom married, Dale and Sharon giving her three grandchildren, and Tom and Jeannine, two. She died on March 21, 1984, at the age of 83.

Pastors Ellen and Dean McGormley, of the Ottawa Presbyterian Church, based Mother's memorial service on the story of Abraham and Sarah and their journey, led by God, to a new land. Pastor Ellen McGormley showed the similarity of that scripture in Genesis to the story of my parents, who also set out on a dangerous journey. They did not know where or when they would reach safety and freedom, but always knew that God was with them, and would show them the way.

"Death, too, is a journey of faith," Pastor Ellen said in her sermon, "and we must trust in God to lead us, just as He has in this life."

Mother did not live to see her son, John, receive a special honor on the fiftieth anniversary of World War II, from the land we had escaped from, but I think she and Papa were chuckling in heaven over the Russian government unknowingly honoring a former Russian citizen, a Mennonite who had once defied them by escaping across the border, at the age of two.

Jake died of cancer in 1989 and Melvin died August 4, 1994. Lydia died of cancer in 1999, and our son, Dale, died of cancer June 6, 2000. My older sister, Helen, is in a nursing home where she sometimes speaks German in her sleep, and still talks with me of the old days in Russia. Helen, John, Alice, and I continue on our faith journey with the legacy of our parents still in our hearts. We gather to honor them as we reminisce on all those years when, just as our little sisters once covered Papa's grave with the warmth of their favorite blanket, our parents covered us with the blanket of God's protection and love.

Tom and me

Tom marries Jeannine Blossom

Melvin and me with Jeannine's parents

Front row, from left, Thomas, Diane, Todd, and James. Middle row, from left, Mike, Melvin, me, and Mother. Top row, from left, Sharon, Dale, Tom, and Jeannine.

John, Helen, me, and Lydia

Front row, Mother. Middle row, from left, me, Alice, Helen, and Myrna. Back row, from left, Melvin, Junior, Dwain, and John.

Amur River & Harbin, China Survivors

Sept. 9, 2001

Schmidt/ Warkentin Reunion in Ottawa, Ohio

John Warkentin, Cornelius (Neil) Schmidt, John Schmidt

Agnes (Warkentin) Rice, Alice (Warkentin) Frey **

Inset: Helen (Warkentin) Hilty *

* Helen was unable to attend due to illness

** Alice was born in Harbin, China

Abram Schmidt (69) died 1989, Peter Schmidt (66) died 1988,

Alice (Liz) Schmidt Sommer (60) died in 1989 (born in Harbin, China)

In Rememberance

Jacob Warkentin (65) died 1989, Lydia Warkentin Mershman (60) died 1999

(Lydia was born in Ohio)

50th Anniversary of the Mennonite Harbin Immigrants Veterans Memorial Building, Dinuba, California, June 22, 1980
Front row, fromleft, Mary (Schmidt) Amstutz, George Warkentin, Ike Warkentin, and Alice (Warkentin) Frey. Top row, from left, Alice (Schmidt) Sommer, John Schmidt, Henry Warkentin, Jacob Warkentin, John Warkentin, Henry Schmidt, John Warkentin, and Helen (Warkentin) Hilty.

Me with Melvin

Alice and Junior Frey

Ebenezer Mennonite Cemetery

Epilogue

Agnes will be 80 in two weeks, or is it 82? She's really not sure, as it's recorded differently in several documents.

"I'm getting younger," she laughs.

She took me to the Mennonite Ebenezer Cemetery last year on a golden day and showed me her Uncle Abe's poem on his gravestone, "The poem he read to us when we parted in Japan," she said.

As we moved on to her parents' graves, and Agnes leaned on the handle bars of her red, three-wheeled walker, or "tricycle," as she calls it, a V-line of geese flew directly over, so low we could see their feet.

"A fly over, Agnes," I said, "for your family and freedom!"

Neta

(Agnes Rice's childhood name)

"Our little Neta is a daily joy"
her father's letter read;
and her faith grew like his.
She worked her needle
through rough cloth
and it made her strong
like her mother.
But still there was time for dancing
to Papa's fiddle,
roller skating with Melvin,
and jokes shared with brothers and sisters
like, "Who broke the window with the ladle?"
She gives a message of tolerance for all,
Russians, Chinese, migrants,
and gleaners of the fields;
and teens listen.
She shows us aging seniors
how to do so gracefully.
From selling corncobs for kindling
to minding her own business,
she shows us how to use our gifts.
She sews some gold
into the seams of each of our lives.

Vera Jones on April 28, 2001

Description Of Our Trip To America

November 7th we left Reinfeld in Slavgorod County on our trip to America. The beginning went well. Our nephew, Gerhard Ewerd, took us to the railroad station by wagon. He also saw us leave and wished us good luck. Our thoughts were already in the big world. We wondered what life might have in store for us.

November the 8th we reached Slavgorod. We boarded the train and were in the same coach with the Abram Schmidts. To the people we said that we were going to the Kuban, but we took a ticket to the Amur. In Tatarsk we changed trains. We two families sat outside the waiting room with our eight children. It was somewhat cool, but no one wanted to go inside, neither children nor grownups.

The 9th of November we boarded the train again and left. We were not on the train very long, only as far as Novosibirsk, and got off again at night. The waiting room was again so full that we could not get in. Then we drove into the city and there we walked around. In the evening we sat again in the train. We had to get a porter, since we had too many things. We paid the cab driver and the porter. Together it was 6 rubles in Novosibirsk.

The evening of November 10th, we left Novosibirsk, in a very nice coach on train number four, third class. We stopped in Irkutsk three hours. Here I sent a telegram to Isaak that he should get us in Blagoveshchensk, and we left.

Then we were traveling toward Batchkorova without trouble. One day before reaching Batchkorova, we stopped for six hours on the steppe, for a train ahead of us had had bad luck. The axle was broken. Thus we reached Batchkorova too late and we had to remain there one day. We reached Batchkorova on November 17th. There we waited one day, left at night and arrived the 18th of November at Blagoveshchensk, and did not find Isaak there. He was not there yet, and there we stood like the oxen before the mountain and did not know what or where. We did not want people to see us, for this would be foolish. We could not do as we wished. So we and the Schmidts went on a wagon to quarters for the night. Then I went to see if I could find Isaak somewhere, but I did not find him anyplace. I waited till evening and then I went again to the peasants' quarters to see whether he had arrived. There were some German people there, but Isaak was not. The people were looking at me. So I left so no one would recognize me. The next day, the 19th of November, I was so tormented by impatience, that I went at once to look again to see if Isaak had arrived. And when I came on to the yard the Germans called to me, "Na, from where do you come? It is good to see you again." I did not know at all what to answer, questions were being asked from all sides. "Are you coming here to live?" "Did you bring your family with you?" What should I say, no or yes? Then I was quiet for a while and thought this over. What should I say, that would help and not be a lie? And then the thought came to me, as it is written, "When the ox falls in the well, so save him, even if it is on Sunday," so I said, "No, I would not drag my family to the Amur. I came alone to put my property in order and then I will go back to my family to the Kuban." (Isaak and a friend found us) and in the evening we left the town in a wagon so no one would see us leave. We and the Schmidts, four big men and two women and eight children on one wagon.

The same thing happened to Isaak. He did not know what to say. As I drove away after speaking to them, everything seemed to be in order. So we drove over the Zeya River and there remained over night. Early in the morning we were up and on our way in a round about way, as if we were going from Bninfa to Pruschup, then to Zamenka and then to the city, so that we would not meet any acquaintances. We drove from morning until evening and we met a Russian whom we knew. Our situation was well known to him. He knew what we wanted. We stayed there overnight. In the morning, the Schmidts stayed there, and we drove to Heinrich's at the border. When we arrived there, it was twelve o'clock at night. They were up and took us in to warm up and to eat. And what was later? We in such misery. What were we to hear? The Amur was not yet completely frozen over. Then we sat and thought about what to do next. We have driven so long, and lied, and all this for nothing. It appears as if it should not be. So we stayed overnight and slept a little. In the morning we were up again and thinking again. And then Heinrich said that Isaak and I should drive home and leave the family there. And so we did. Heinrich had a brother by the name of Johan, a good and brave boy. And so he and another boy named Schmitz and Heinrich, took the two girls by the hand and went over by day. And when they knew that both girls were over the border, Heinrich took the rest of the family over by night, he and his brother, Jakob, and a Wiebe from Nikolaipol, district of Slavgorod. One took my Jakob, the other took Johan, and the third took two tablecloths (of things). Then mother followed after the two boys. How dark and troubled a time it is, when there is no other way, only forward!

The next day, the 23rd of November, I went back to Heinrich's, to see if everything went well with my family. When I arrived at Heinrich's, they were not yet back from the other side and the women folk cried. There was not yet any news from them whether they arrived happily or had the ice broken, and they were all somewhere under the ice? So I stayed a while and then the men came back with a letter from the girls, saying that they all arrived and were well received. So I thought about Noah when he opened the window to let doves out and they came back with an olive leaf — so it was with the letter. So I pondered for a while and wondered what would happen. My family across the water without me, among strangers with whom they could not speak. I stayed with Isaak for six days, always uncertain, imagining that someone was behind me. I will never feel well until I have the ones that belong to me again before my eyes. So I sold my property in Amur for 120 rubles and took the money and drove away from Shimanovsk as if I would go to the Kuban. I drove ten *vierst* and then turned and drove to Heinrich's. I drove with white horses that I left at Isaak's until evening. When I arrived at Heinrich's, I stayed there over night. The next day I hitched up my white horses to a sleigh and with Heinrich in his sleigh pulled by brown horses by my side, we went over the border. Because the ice was weak that morning, one took the gun, the other had two straw ticks and one comforter in the sleigh, everything was covered with straw. We tied the chamber pot on the front of the sled and we added the axe and skunk traps, so in case someone would see us, they would not suspect what we had in mind. And as for my money, I did not have the 2,000 rubles with me, and the rest of the things we left with Heinrich. Some of the things were already sold: the shoes, the boots, a blanket, and four pillows. In crossing the border everything is too much. Happily I crossed the border with my white horses and I spent the night by the border. The next day I went into the mountains to meet my family. The trip was slow and jolting. But I arrived and found everybody alive. But if you, my brothers and sisters would see how we live, you would open your eyes. "How can you do it?" But when one is on a journey one must accommodate one's self to everything. What we wanted to buy was expensive. For 1 Russian ruble, you get so little. For 1 ruble you get 40 to 50 kopecks. Flour costs, in their money, 3 rubels a pound, meat 20 to 30 kopecks a pound, and fish 10 kopecks a pound and so everything you wanted to buy in their money. According to our money, everything is very expensive. In case there is no change, then our trip would look very sad. I shall see tomorrrow whether I can bring some more things over. When one has littlc, it is sad, but when one has nothing it is worse. When we crossed the border our possessions were only people and children. But we do not want to lose hope, but only go forward.

The 4th of December we went again over the border. Jakob Wiebe from Nikolaipol and I got the things that we had left at Heinrich's. In walking, we thought about many things. Why does it have to be this way; why did we start this trip? We cannot understand what good can come out of this. And yet, brothers and sisters, all has gone well so far, even though it looked very troublesome sometimes. And when all is said and done, we must say that our great God is with us here also. We are sometimes in a position that we have to think of the kindness of God. Now my brothers and sisters and acquaintances, you will think that it had happened to me in order to know that the fork sits on the handle. "His life was too good for him so far, so he had to choose to leave." Now brothers and sisters, I shall not forget this as long as I live. And when I arrive where I plan to be, I shall be satisfied. I would advise no one to do the same. The whole thing is like a chess game. When one has luck, he has luck and when not, everything is lost. I imagined that the trip would be terrible, but if I had known it to be so difficult with a family, then I would not have done it. In summer, when I was in Amur alone, it was not difficult.

But now we have lacked nothing and all went well; we are together with the children and with Heinrich, the Schmitz boy, and Jacob Wiebe, and are healthy. We are living here in this Chinese village like ghosts. On the Russian side I still have 2,000 rubles which someone will bring to me on Sunday and if not, then I shall return to get the money myself. Then I will also go to town for papers so that we are free to travel to China. When we have the papers, we will go to Harbin and begin to work on plans to go to America. I sold my white horse for 65 rubles in Chinese money, which would be 130 rubles in Russian money. So we have enough to live. I hoped the Russian exchange would be better. Last year the same happened in the fall. After the New Year, the Russian money exchange should be higher. When this is the case, we shall again live better. If we did not have hope, we would not live anymore. So all depends on our hope. The time now is not for us. We hope soon to meet the Schmidts. We are two-and-a-half weeks apart, and so we must have patience.

Today is the 6th of December. We have nothing to do but eat and sleep and stand by the stove. I often think of Abram Friesen; how comfortable he had it. Nothing to do only to eat and stand by the stove. In my case, my wife does not run around in the village and beg food. The providing of food is my business. So the thoughts travel back and forth, from Siberia to China, always back and forth. It is good that I do not have to pay for the trips that are in my thoughts. I would be without money already.

Today for dinner we had gruel (groat), and substitute coffee, and bread. It is simple enough but we survive. And the children are just as mischievous as at home. The communal life is a simple life. One does not hear anything about prayer or talking with God. They are like the Karchensen (nomads of Siberia), only they have better housing. They also eat pork. They have no rules about food. But each morning they bake fresh, only enough for the day. To me, they are all like ravens, the people as well as the food, everything the same. Their faces and clothes look alike. What a big difference compared to Russia. Life was different there. To live here like they do, then it is better to die.... They even are happy. It is sad what they make from flour. It is cooked like *kilgen* (thick noodles or dumplings as big as a fist). The men make the meals. They arise early, make a fire and begin to prepare the meals. For breakfast they have dumplings and a mixture of vegetables that cannot be determined. And they do not eat with a fork or spoon but with wooden sticks. It looks very sad. In the evening, soup is cooked again and the leftover dumplings. They eat only twice a day. During the day, a kettle of tea is always ready. Whoever is hungry goes and drinks tea. Bread as we know it is unknown here, the dumplings they call *pepushka*. We that crossed the border first, have the most to suffer. But people are very hospitable.

Today, we have nice sunshine and we are in a warm room. I am thinking of the expenses I had in Russia until we came to the border. The ticket — 110 rubles, wagons till Slavgorad — 5 rubles, then we lived through the whole journey with good food, the cabdriver, the porter — it all amounts to 45 rubles. Then I gave Isaak money for bringing us from the city and taking us to Heinrich, to cross the border — 45 rubels. And now, good-bye, Russia. No money nor soldiers will we give you; we will live in a different way in freedom where all men have their own free will. No one will take advantage of us and it will be a joy to live. The expense for the entire journey was 205 rubles. Good-bye, U.S.S.R. Even here we keep the right to vote, not only Uncle Kreiger and Father Alexander Hamm. Today the 8th of December, even with all our wandering we had something to laugh about.

There is a very special grandmother with a long pipe, one arshin long, which she holds in her mouth constantly, even when working. These people were very strange to us.

Yesterday, the 11th of December, I got the Schmidts from the border. They came with Heinrich on foot unobserved by any soldier. I went to meet them a long distance and helped them carry the children. Anna was stiff from walking as it was about six *vierst* up the hill and down again and it had to be done quickly. When this was all over, everyone was so tired; all they thought about was sleep. My family went over the border November 20, so this family came twenty days later. Abe had to stay in Kotolashke, so that no one would see him. I am sorry that Heinrich could not come along. It would have been simple without children. Or Peter Nachtigal, he also had enough money saved up that he could have traveled with me to the Kuban, and it would have been a little more sociable. So far everything has gone well.

We have gotten letters from Johann Gossen in answer to the ones I wrote last summer. He tells us that we can come to America, which gives us much consolation. We also wrote to the Schulzes in America.

December 19th. We were three days on the road to the village, Katchuriga for the documents. We sent our landlord and Heinrich to the city for permission to go to live in Harbin. I went to get 1,000 rubles from the other side. Now I have all my money with me except for 500 rubles. Everyone is healthy and alive. We and the Abram Schmidts in one room. Together eighteen souls. It is full like a beehive and what noise! But we hope always for a different life. I sold leather in China for Isaak for 75 kopecks Chinese money. With our money we can do little among the farmers. Abram Schmidt and I wanted to go to the store on December 24th. As we were on the way there, the two from the city came by car and brought us the documents to go to Harbin. So we took them and drove with the car to Eigu where we had to wait three days. Then we drove to Zagalon where we changed the money. Then we drove back to our families. It was just around Christmas and we again took the car and drove to Trebek. (We took a bus to Tsitsihar.) Then we took the train to Harbin. There was much to do, but it was all accomplished.

New Year's Eve we were in Harbin. We celebrated Christmas here in Harbin in the old customary way. So we had much to do. We didn't have much, but we let Santa Claus come. So it gave us also in Harbin some joy even if only a little one. So life in Harbin is pretty good. Only money is worth so little. 50 kopecks for a ruble. The expenses always double. Flour costs from 3.50 to 4 rubles, sugar 25 kopecks, sugarcandy 15 kopecks, bread 6 kopecks, groats 7 kopecks, white bread 7 kopecks, butter 38 kopecks, lard 45 kopecks, meat 20 kopecks, and bacon 45 kopecks. That is the cost of the products. As far as dry goods, they are cheap and good. Good woven long underwear for myself 3 rubles, a blanket better than in Russia was 15 kopecks there, here 4 rubles, and so it goes.

October 3, 1929, We left Harbin to go to America, and on October 11th we went on board the ship. On October 15th, we did not count one day, so we had two October 16ths in order to be in step with American time.

Praise and glory to the Lord
That He has led us so well
No enemy has seen us
The scales were weighed toward peace
Yes, the Lord has led us, this we believe.
We lived with the Asiatics
Were looked at from all sides
As though they will devour us.
In peace and quiet
After we thought about the past
We left behind us.

How wonderful everything went!
and still goes on today
No one had to hunger
To eat, there was enough
The same it was with the wise woman
Whose pitcher never got empty.
But finally it happened
What we had always wished
The golden land to walk on
About which the whole world speaks
And absolved from all our sorrow,
Which still rules over you there.
Halleluia, good hope. Amen.

According to the old style:
Our wedding was August 10, 1918
Aron Warkentin was born April 24, 1898
Aganetha Wiebe was born September 19, 1900
Daughters:
Helene was born October 18, 1919
Aganetha was born April 28, 1922
Elsa was born February 16, 1929

Sons:

Aron was born May 6, 1920 and died July 10, 1920
Gehard was born March 27, 1924 and died April 7, 1924
Jakob was born April 14, 1925
Johan was born March 27, 1927

Added by Aganetha Warkentin (my mother)

Aron and I werc both born in Holland to German Mennonite parents and our families immigrated into South Eastern Russia in 1900, on land that Russia had opened to be settled. We lived in a Mennonite community which consisted of five villages. We had our own churches, schools, etc. We all farmed and grew wheat, oats, and rye, and raised livestock. The winters were very cold, degrees as low as 40 below zero, the temperature fell lower than at the North Pole, but since the air was dry we didn't mind the cold. Summer temperatures didn't get over 65 degrees. We had a very short growing season, but everything grew well. Vegetable gardens were very good. My father was a doctor and this new settlement was a challenge to him. I was 8 months old when we moved to Russia. In 1905, the Revolution started. Social Democrats and Socialist leaders gradually gained control under the rule of Lenin. In 1918, a civil war broke out between the Bolsheviks (Reds) and the Mensheviks (Whites). Aron was in the medical corps in this war. This was followed up by World War I, Russia fought against Germany under Lenin's rule. By 1922, many people starved to death in Russia (7,000,000). The economy started going down because of the wars and the depressed people of Russia. Food supplies were sent to Russia from the United States by the NEP (New Economic Policy). Herbert Hoover was president at this time.

This is when the Russian government made the farmers give their crops over to them. Farmers were allowed to keep just a fixed amount of grain regardless of the size of their families. We buried much grain because they would not let us keep enough to feed our family. Later we would dig it up, and helped many people in the village who didn't have enough to eat. We saw many of our neighbors starve to death. In 1924, Stalin took over leadership after Lenin's death. Churches were destroyed because they considered them an obstruction to Communism. All religious literature and Bibles were burned if they could get hold of them.

Aron and I were married August 10th, 1918. To this union eight children were born, six are living. Six children were born in Russia, one in China, and one in America.

In the summer of 1928, Aron and Isaak Warkentin, his brother, went to Amur, (a village on the banks of the Amur River which we crossed), and built a small frame house in preparation for our flight out of Russia. Isaak and his family moved into the house to make the Communists think he was just going to move.

The Schmidts, the Warkentins, and we would not sign up to join the Communist Party so things were very rough for us. We knew we had to leave or they would shoot us or put us into concentration camps. On November 7th, 1928, arrangements had been made between the three families, that we could leave. We sold as much of our belongings as we could without suspicion. I sewed our money into the hems of the children's clothes so nobody could find it, in case we would be stopped.

It took a month in Harbin for Aron to locate the American Consulate. Here he got in contact with a German doctor who had gone to college with a Mennonite minister by the name of Reverend Regere who was a minister in a large Mennonite church in Reedley, California. This doctor wrote to Reverend Regere and told him our plight, wanting to get into the United States and needing a sponsor. They accepted us and we knew we could come. The quota was filled into the United States for 7 months so we lived in Harbin until we could leave. Alice was born during this time, with no assistance of a doctor, only Aron. Alice was 7 months old when we left Harbin to go to America, on the *S. Asoma Maru*. Helen and Agnes got very sick on the ship. We landed in San Francisco and were put on Angel Island where they screened all immigrants. Again, the girls and I were separated from Aron and the boys, and I again wondered if we would see each other again. But after three days we were again united and were shipped across the bay to San Francisco. Here Reverend Regere met us and our life could begin.

They supplied for us. Helen got seasick in bed the first night because the beds were too soft for her. When we left Russia we had approximately $5,550 in American money. When we landed in the States we had $47 left over.

Aron did not like the irrigation they used in California to do their farming. This he wasn't used to. We picked grapes and other fruit to make a living.

Dr. Mosiman from Bluffton College came to California to visit Reverend Regere, who had been the minister of the Grace Mennonite Church in Pandora, Ohio, for eight years. He told Dr. Mosiman about us wanting to get work on a farm. Bluffton College had just acquired 450 acres of farm land in Washington Court House, Ohio. The college sent for us, and we came to Ohio to work that farm.

The Schmidts and the Isaak Warkentins landed in Seattle, Washington, when they came to the States. Aron wrote to them and told them we were going to Ohio. So all the families got together again and we all made the trip together. The

Schmidts were put on a farm in Beaverdam, Ohio. The Isaak Warkentins and we were put in a home near Beaverdam until the farm home in Washington Court House was ready for us. It was an old brick house; the Warkentins had the upstairs and we were down.

This was November 2, 1930, and Lydia was born in Bluffton Hospital on November 27th. Isaak did not like it here so they went back to Seattle. We moved to Washington Court House March 1, 1931.

Aron was injured in a farm accident and only lived a short while. He died December 19, 1932, and was buried December 21, 1932; so he did not live long enough to fulfill the great dream that he had. We then moved to the Pandora area so we could be closer to the Schmidts. I had six children to raise, and it was hard, but with the grace of God and a lot of hard work, we made it. Aron gave his family a great opportunity to have a better life.

Isaak Warkentin died April 1934
Abram Schmidt died Oct. 19, 1935
Anna Schmidt died Nov. 28, 1955

Aron, Abram, and Anna are buried at the Ebenezer Cemetery near Bluffton, Ohio.

Bibliography

Newspaper articles

Obituaries of Aron Warkentin, Agnes Wiebe Warkentin, and Abram Schmidt.

Obituary of Myrna Warkentin, (The *Toledo Blade*, Aug. 30, 2002).

Article, "Flight from Russia," (The *Gilboa Gazette*, Feb., 1981).

Article, "Senior Citizen of the Year," (*Putnam County Sentinel*, May 5, 1999).

Journal of the American Historical Society of Germans from Russia, Vol. 10, #2, Summer, 1987, by Katie Michelson Melvin.

Books

The Bible.

Journey into China, published by the National Geographic Society, Washington, D.C., 1982.

Great Rivers of the World, National Geographic Society, Washington, D.C., 1984.

Magazine articles

"Siberia's Empire Road, The River Ob" by Robert Paul Jordan, photographer, Dean Conger, *National Geographic*, Feb., 1976.

"China Passage by Rail," by Paul Theroux, photographer, Bruce Dale, *National Geographic*, Mar., 1988.

"Siberia in from the Cold," by Mike Edwards, photographer, Steve Raymer; and "Last Days of the Gulag," by Jean-Pierre Vaudon, photographer, Pierre Perrin, *National Geographic*, Mar., 1990.

"Black Dragon River" by Simon Winchester, photographer, Reza, *National Geographic*, Feb., 2000.

Vera Jones graduated from Oberlin College, Oberlin, Ohio, and has taught elementary and junior high school children in Illinois, Ohio, and Iran. She has traveled in Europe, the Middle East, and the United States, and has been a writer most of her life. She has won a number of prizes in the Ohio Poetry Day Contests, and had several articles published in small magazines. This is her first book.